PAINLESS
Research
Projects

Rebecca Elliott, Ph.D. and James Elliott, M.A.
illustrated by Laurie Hamilton

BARRON'S

All inquiries should be addressed to:
Barron's Educational Series, Inc.
250 Wireless Boulevard
Hauppauge, New York 11788
http://www.barronseduc.com.

International Standard Book No. 0-7641-0297-4

Library of Congress Catalog Card No. 97-48597

Library of Congress Cataloging-in-Publication Data

Elliott, Rebecca, 1948–
     Painless research projects / Rebecca Elliott and James Elliott.
        p.   cm.
     Includes index.
     Summary: Provides step-by-step instructions for writing an
interesting and informative research paper, from choosing a topic to
proofreading the finished product.
     ISBN 0-7641-0297-4
     1. Report writing—Juvenile literature.   2. Research—Juvenile
literature. [1. Report writing. 2. Research.]   I. Elliott,
James, 1953–   . II. Title
LB1047.3.E55   1998
372.6—dc21   97-48597
                                                        CIP
                                                         AC

PRINTED IN THE UNITED STATES OF AMERICA
9 8 7 6 5 4 3 2

We dedicate this book to our parents

Acknowledgments

Research is a process of learning from other people, thinking up ideas and discovering things on your own, and weaving it all together in your own unique way. It is very rare that you can do an A+ research project all by yourself—usually you need to ask for help from teachers, librarians, parents, friends, and others. We asked for a lot of help in writing this book. We thank these people for their advice and support: James Davis, Judy Knight, Marjorie Lancaster, Carolyn Parker, Carolyn Peterson, Carol Rogers, Angela Short, and the librarians at the Chapel Hill, North Carolina, public library. Special thanks to our very helpful readers and editors: Jim Clark, Cheryl Farnbaugh, Donna Gulick, Marshall McCorkle, Heather Miller, Mike Smith, Bill Stevens, Amy Van Allen, and Carolyn White.

CONTENTS

INTRODUCTION

Some students feel that research projects are a sneaky plot by teachers to torture innocent students. That's not exactly true. Research projects are a sneaky plot by teachers to show kids how to think creatively, discover interesting information, and use that information in exciting ways.

If you think about it, you've probably done a lot of research without ever realizing it. Depending on your interests, you may have read everything you could get your hands on about dinosaurs or your favorite movie star or sports hero. When you were gathering that information, you were conducting research. Research is a lot of fun when you're curious about the topic you're studying. One of the things this book will show you is that learning how to do research will help you in life both in school and outside school. Here's how:

> Imagine that you are about to turn 18 and have saved enough money to buy a used car. If you don't do any research, you might spend all your hard-earned money on a car with a reputation for breaking down all the time. Armed with the right research, you could figure out how to get the best car for your money. Which car dealers in town have the best reputations? Which car models last the longest? What problems do older Fords have? What about older Mazdas, Chevrolets, and other cars that interest you? What are fair prices for these cars? What questions should you ask the dealer about the particular car you like? What mechanic should you ask to check the car, and how would you know if he or she is giving you a good evaluation? How much does car insurance cost? How do you go about getting insurance? How do you get a license plate for your new car?
>
> And what if your grandfather says he will give you $500 toward your car if you write him a long letter telling him what you learned. Would you write that $500 letter? Yes? Well, then you just wrote a painless research report.

Let's look at another example.

When you're in high school you get a summer job in a clothing store. Your boss is very impressed that you are selling more clothes to teenagers than any other salesperson in the store. She wants to know what to buy for the store and asks your opinion on the hottest new trends in teenage fashion. You could just tell her what you would buy, or you could do some research. Check the teen magazines—not just one of them, but three or four. See what types of clothes that different magazines are showing. Look for articles in those magazines about national fashion trends. Talk to several of your best-dressed friends and ask them what they like. Ask them why they like that style, where they buy their clothes, what fashions they think are out of style, and what styles they think or hope will be popular soon. Call the national headquarters of companies such as Gap or Benetton, tell them your project, and ask if they have catalogs or publicity brochures that they could send you about their latest styles.

Put all this information together in a lively way that your boss will enjoy, add a colorful collage of fashion photos, and guess what? You have just written and illustrated a research paper—one that just might get you a raise.

It doesn't matter what you want to know more about: cars or fashion; antique dolls, race horses, or military airplanes; the history of the Internet, how Native Americans helped early settlers in your town, or a million other subjects. No matter what you research, there are techniques and tips, strategies and styles that are always effective.

This book will teach you how it's done—the painless way.

Your search for treasure

Doing a research project is a lot like going on a treasure hunt. This book maps out all the steps. Chapter One shows you how to get ready for your search. It covers choosing a clear research topic and deciding exactly how you're going to turn that topic into gold.

Chapter Two is about getting into the thick of research and digging for your treasure. In this chapter you learn how to use the library to uncover the information you're seeking.

Chapter Three takes your treasure hunt on new and exciting paths—through the amazing mass of information on the World Wide Web!

Chapter Four shows you how to find interesting information for your research through interviews, questionnaires, and other often-overlooked resources.

Chapter Five shows you how to take notes on all the information you find.

Chapter Six teaches you how to sort through your notes and get your treasure ready to show to the world (or at least to your teacher) by writing a paper.

Even treasure can be a little dusty or tarnished. In Chapter Seven, you learn about shining your gold and silver—cleaning up your paper until it sparkles. Then Chapter Eight takes you step-by-step through a sample research report.

At the end of the book are three appendices filled with valuable information. Appendix A has helpful checklists to use as you progress through your research projects. Appendix B gives you blank forms to help when doing bibliographies. Appendix C lists several Internet sites and describes how they can be useful for researching various topics.

It's our hope that this trip will be packed with fun for you. We want to show you how to do research in a way that makes your imagination sizzle, not fizzle, how to uncover the hottest information about things that matter to you, and how to present that information in a clear, exciting way.

Now, let the search begin!

CHAPTER ONE

Starting Your Treasure Hunt

Your teacher has assigned a research project. That means you are about to go on a treasure hunt, looking for some valuable information. Once you have found that information, you will organize it and present your new knowledge so that others can share in it. Most often you will be asked to write a paper, but sometimes your teacher might want you to put on a play, make a poster, write a song, build a model, prepare a feast or festival, or draw pictures or maps. No matter how you show off your treasure, the process of finding it is the same. There's treasure out there! Let's get started.

PICKING A TOPIC

First, you need an idea for a project. What are you going to research? Often your teacher will assign a general topic and let you choose the focus that appeals to you most. Other times your teacher will allow you to pick any topic that interests you. Either way, you have to do some thinking. You also get to have some fun! Here are some examples of creative and interesting ways to come up with ideas for your research.

- **Listen carefully** in class as your teacher explains things. Listen to your parents' and friends' conversations. Is there something that excites your curiosity—something you would like to know more about? Write down that idea.

YOUR TEACHER SAYS:
"I prefer clocks with digital displays."
YOU GET THIS IDEA:
Who invented the first mechanical timepiece and how was that clock used?

YOUR FRIEND SAYS:
"Tomorrow I can't eat all day because it's Yom Kippur."
YOU GET THIS IDEA:
What other religions besides Judaism celebrate their holy days by fasting (not eating)?

YOUR GRANDPA SAYS:
"I remember when cars didn't have automatic transmissions."
YOU GET THIS IDEA:
Are scientists working on technology that would make it possible for cars of the future to be driven by robots?

YOUR MOM SAYS:
"Wash your hands before you eat."
YOU GET THIS IDEA:
What would my life be like if I were a germ?

- **Ask for ideas** from your teachers, parents, friends, or school librarian. Listen closely to what they say. Pretend their ideas are clay, then mold that clay into your own idea for a project.

YOUR MOM SUGGESTS:
"Write about jets."
YOU GET THIS IDEA:
What's the difference between a jet engine and a car engine?

YOUR GRANDMOTHER SUGGESTS:
"Write about children in Africa."
YOU GET THIS IDEA:
How do organizations like UNICEF help sick children in Africa?

- **General interest magazines** are packed with good ideas. There are many excellent magazines in the library and on the newsstand. Here are a few:

  Smithsonian Magazine
  Newsweek
  National Geographic
  Time
  Discover

- **Magazines related to your hobbies** will contain ideas that interest you. These might be good magazines to check out:

  Sports Illustrated for Kids
  Popular Photography
  Seventeen
  Horse and Rider
  Popular Science
  Road and Track

- **Questions about your hobbies** could point you in an interesting direction.

  Has the in-line skating craze spread around the world?
  What are the oldest musical instruments?
  How are funny mistakes sometimes made in the printing of
    U.S. postage stamps?

- **Look through the reference books** in the library or a good book store. You'll find reference books on sports, animals, science, fashion, music, foreign countries, inventions, warplanes—lots of interesting subjects. Take down a few books and flip through them until you see a topic that appeals to you.

- **Watch television news shows** like *60 Minutes* or the various news channels for ideas about exciting current events.

  "The Presidential Elections: How They Affect Kids"
  "Will We Send Astronauts to Mars?"
  "Will the Internet Replace Television?"

- **Think of an interesting person** you would like to know more about.

  "The Musical Contributions of Stevie Wonder"
  "Albert Einstein Was a Great Philosopher as Well as a Scientist"
  "Rosa Parks and Her Courageous Role in the Civil Rights Movement"

- **Think about an important issue in your town** that you think would be interesting. Look through your local newspaper for stories.

  "Recent Discoveries About the Native Americans Who Lived near My Hometown 300 Years Ago"
  "Differences between Mayoral Candidates Jones and Smith in Their Views on Making the School Year 11 Months Long"
  "The Hot Debate in Our Town about Allowing High School Students to Leave Campus for Lunch"

- **Watch the world around you.** Notice people doing things that seem unusual, animals that you don't recognize, people celebrating holidays that are different from your own, or objects in the sky you've never noticed before. Most of your best ideas will come from the life you experience right around you. If an idea excites you, grab it. Write it down so you won't forget, and later decide whether you can turn it into a project that your teacher will approve.

Tip

This is how professional writers get their ideas. They look and listen for little things that interest them, jot them down, and later turn those little ideas into short articles, long articles, even books. The pros get started on their projects exactly the same way you are getting started on yours.

This topic is too big

Imagine that your teacher says, "I want you to write a five-page report on the history of the world." Oh, no! That means you have to write everything about *everything in the world* in five pages. Fortunately, your teacher is kidding. What he really wants is for you to pick one tiny sliver of the history of the world and learn a lot about it.

Would you like to do a research report on sports? That sounds like fun, but if you don't narrow down that huge topic, your paper will be about a billion pages long. That would take a mighty long time for you to type. Let's see how to tame a monstrous topic.

TOO BIG:
  "Sports"
MORE SPECIFIC:
  "Women in Sports"
EVEN MORE SPECIFIC:
  "Women's Gymnastics"
MANAGEABLE:
  "The History of Women's Gymnastics"

Here's another example of putting a titanic topic on a diet.

TOO BIG:
   "The United States of America"
MORE SPECIFIC:
   "My State"
EVEN MORE SPECIFIC:
   "My Town"
EVEN MORE SPECIFIC:
   "The Government of My Town"
MANAGEABLE:
   "The Mayor of My Town"

This topic is too small

If you decide to do a report on the sneezing habits of baby penguins, you will have a big problem on your hands. Where on earth are you going to find information on such a tiny subject? Your school library probably doesn't have professional science journals. You surely don't have time to fly to Antarctica to do the research yourself, and you probably don't have a big sister who studies penguins for a living.

Be careful not to focus so narrowly that there's no information available. If you like an idea but discover that it's too tiny when you start your research, don't throw the idea into the trash. Just make it a little bigger. Let's see how that works:

TOO TINY:
   "Sneezing Habits of Baby Penguins"
BIGGER AND BETTER:
   "How Baby Penguins Survive in Such Cold Climates"

<u>TOO TINY:</u>
"The Favorite Color of Bumblebees"

<u>BIGGER AND BETTER:</u>
"How Nature Uses Color to Attract Insects to Pollinate Plants"

IS THIS TOPIC AS EASY TO RESEARCH AS IT LOOKS?

Before you rush to the library, think about whether your project is going to be easy to research or very difficult to research. Some topics that sound like lots of fun can be a mountain of work. That's fine if you love the topic (in fact, it's great), but be sure you have enough time to do the research.

<u>SOUNDS EASY:</u>
"The Civil Rights Movement in My Town in 1968"

<u>HARD TO RESEARCH UNLESS:</u>
Your school library has the local newspaper with an index going back to 1968.

<u>OR:</u>
You're willing to go to the city library to do most of your research.

<u>SOUNDS EASY:</u>
"How Laser Surgery Works"

<u>HARD TO RESEARCH UNLESS:</u>
You are very good at science and like to read sophisticated scientific journals.

<u>OR:</u>
Someone you know can help you understand the very technical information this project would involve.

Don't get too discouraged if you discover that information on your topic is not available, is very hard to find, or is too technical for you to understand. If you hit a dead end, it's not your fault. In fact, it's a sign of good research to discover early that there really isn't any treasure down that road after all. All famous scientists and researchers hit dead ends now and then, but they don't give up. They say, "Now I know that approach doesn't work," and they begin to look around for another approach or another idea that will work.

Think of Jonas Salk (he discovered the polio vaccine), Thomas Edison (he gave us light bulbs and movie cameras), and Josephine Cochrane (she gave us the first mechanical dishwasher). If those researchers had given up when they hit dead ends, our world would be a very different place today. When you get frustrated, rest a little bit, then head off in a new, more hopeful direction.

This topic is just right

What makes a topic just right?

Size

It's not too huge and it's not too tiny.

TOO HUGE:
"Dogs"

TOO TINY:
"Left Paw Fungus Problems of Poodles in Patagonia"

JUST RIGHT:
"How Dogs Are Used on Farms and Ranches"

Simplicity

The information you need to read is neither way over your head nor way too easy.

PROBABLY OVER YOUR HEAD:
> "The Biochemistry behind the Latest Medicines for Treating Pneumonia"

NO CHALLENGE AT ALL:
> "Why *Pneumonia* Is Spelled Funny"

JUST RIGHT:
> "What Is Pneumonia and How Is It Cured?"

Access

Information about the topic is not terribly hard to find.

HARD-TO-FIND INFORMATION:
> "The Favorite Foods of the First Five U.S. Presidents"

EASY-TO-FIND INFORMATION:
> "The Biggest Accomplishments of the First Five U.S. Presidents"

Interest

The topic is interesting to you or, if it's boring, you have figured out a way to put an interesting twist on it.

BORING:
> "Trends in the U.S. Economy"

INTERESTING TWIST:
> "Teenage Entrepreneurs Who Founded Successful Businesses"

BRAIN TICKLERS
Set #1

Research should be fun, but it always takes a little planning. You'll have more fun flying a kite on a day that is forecast to be windy rather than calm, and you'll have more fun if you check your tennis racket for broken strings before you start hitting.

It's the same with research. Before you put a lot of time and effort into a topic, think about problems you might encounter. What problems can you see with these topics?

1. "Martin Luther King, Jr."

2. "One or Two Facts about the Play Habits of Three-Day-Old Bengal Tigers"

3. "The 1970 Citywide Outcry When the Local School Board Threatened to Suspend Students for Wearing Culottes"

4. "Favorite Hobbies of Teachers in Our School"

5. "Essential Minerals in the Diet of Baboons"

6. "Endangered Animals"

(Answers on page 32.)

PLANNING HOW TO PRESENT YOUR PROJECT

Once you have a topic, think about the best way to present it to your teacher or to your class. If your topic is about the Empire State Building, you might want to build a model. If you are researching different types of eagles, you will probably want to include drawings or photographs. You might change your mind about your presentation as you uncover information about your topic, but having an idea of how you will present your material gives you a very good idea of what type of material to search for.

Let's look at a few examples of good ways and not-so-good ways to present information.

TOPIC:
the life of a famous artist

GOOD PRESENTATION:
a paper describing the artist's life

GOOD PRESENTATION:
a skit or short play about the artist's life

NOT-SO-GOOD PRESENTATION:
a collage of his or her paintings
(The topic is the artist's life, not just his or her work.)

NOT-SO-GOOD PRESENTATION:
maps of the area where this artist lived
(Maps probably don't tell much about the artist's life.)

TOPIC:
the rise and decline of the British Empire

GOOD PRESENTATION:
a timeline with maps showing sailing routes and maps of
the countries that became part of the empire

GOOD PRESENTATION:
a paper describing in brief what occurred over several
hundred years of English colonial rule

NOT-SO-GOOD PRESENTATION:
a model of an 18th-century British ship
(Ships were involved in British exploration and colonization,
but even a well-built model of a ship doesn't give
enough information about the topic.)

NOT-SO-GOOD PRESENTATION:
a homemade video
(How are you going to be able to get film footage of
things that happened several hundred years ago?)

As you do more research projects, it gets easier to decide exactly how to present your topic. In the meantime, use your imagination to come up with as many ideas as you can and ask your teacher to help you choose the one that's best.

Knowing what your teacher wants

It's wise at this point to take a very important time out. Be sure to carefully read your teacher's instructions. The first step in doing an A+ research project is knowing what you are expected to do. If you aren't clear about the instructions, you'll never get off to an A+ start.

Sometimes kids do outstanding work but get low grades for not following instructions. If you know exactly what you are expected to do, it will save you lots of time and will make your task much easier and much more rewarding.

Caution! Major mistake territory!

Students sometimes misunderstand or misread directions for projects. If your teacher wants you to research bears and you learn a lot about pears—oops! Ask as many questions as you need in order to be sure you're clear about what your teacher wants.

Here are some things you should pay very close attention to:

Approach

Does your teacher want you to take a particular approach to this project? If he had wanted you to write about why we should protect blue whales and you wrote about how Eskimos hunt for whales, you'd be off track. You might have written a wonderful paper, but you didn't follow instructions, and your teacher would not be pleased.

Imagine that your teacher wants a research project on the American Civil War. These topics would be right on the money:

ON-TRACK TOPIC:
"How Slaves Were Sneaked to Freedom on the Underground Railroad"

ON-TRACK TOPIC:
"Famous Civil War Battlefields in My State"

But these topics would not meet your teacher's guidelines:

OFF-TRACK TOPIC:
"My Great-Great-Grandfather's Special Mission in the Spanish Civil War"

OFF-TRACK TOPIC:
"Clothing Fashions in the South Prior to the Civil War"

Imagine that your teacher wants a research report about the childhood of your favorite author. These ideas would be right on the money:

ON-TRACK TOPIC:
"Was Mark Twain's Childhood Similar to Huck Finn's?"

ON-TRACK TOPIC:
"Did Stephen King Have a Scary Childhood?"

But these would not meet your teacher's guidelines:

OFF-TRACK TOPIC:
"Are Stephen King Books Too Scary for Children?"

OFF-TRACK TOPIC:
"My Favorite Poems About Childhood"

Length

How long should this paper be? If your teacher wants five pages and you write 55, you will not be the teacher's pet. If she wants ten pages, don't expect an A+ if you turn in two pages. It's usually okay to be a page or two over, even a little under if your report is good, but don't be too far off the mark.

Deadline

What is the deadline for this project? Are you expected to turn in an outline or a rough draft before the final deadline? If so, when? There's nothing worse than finding out you forgot a deadline—and it's *tomorrow!* Write down all those deadline dates.

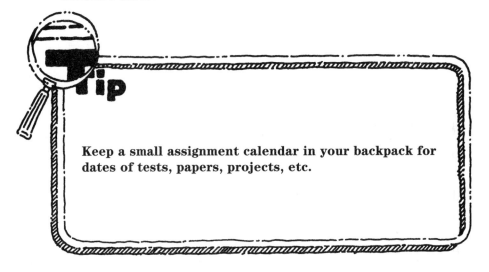

Tip

Keep a small assignment calendar in your backpack for dates of tests, papers, projects, etc.

Type of presentation

If your presentation is going to be something other than a paper, clear your ideas with your teacher. (Is a big poster okay? A series of maps? A short piece of historical fiction?) If your teacher has assigned something other than a paper, be sure you know what she expects. If you are assigned to do a skit with other class members, which classmates are your team members? Do you need costumes? If you are going to make a poster, what size should it be? If you are going to create a cardboard model of a dinosaur, what scale will it be?

(It would take an awful lot of cardboard to make a full-size display of a Tyrannosaurus!)

Number of sources

How many sources of information (books, newspapers, magazines, encyclopedias, interviews, Internet sites, etc.) does your teacher want you to use? Usually middle school teachers ask for three or four, but you need to be sure. If your teacher says you must have three sources, don't stop at two. If you're excited about your subject and you want to look it up in a fourth book, go for it. The more places you dig for information, the better.

Writing or typing

Is it okay for your paper to be handwritten? Does it need to be typed? If so, is a typewriter okay or must your paper be done on a computer?

Graphics

Do you need to include pictures, maps, drawings, or diagrams? If so, do you need to draw them yourself or is it okay to photo-copy pictures or cut pictures out of brochures or magazines? Is it okay to use a computer scanner and printouts?

Special guidelines

When your teacher gives you guidelines about how to do title pages, footnotes, or bibliographies, put that information in a place where you can easily find it when it's time to prepare those parts of your report.

BRAIN TICKLERS
Set #2

1. Allison's science teacher assigns the class a research project on some aspect of winter weather. Allison decides to write about the hurricane that roared through her town last year. What advice would you give Allison?

2. The teacher wants a report about how a particular animal has adapted to its environment in some special way. Sam writes a report about how seeing-eye dogs are trained to help blind people. Can you see how Sam is off track?

(Answers on page 33.)

Imagining your topic's possibilities

Now that you have a topic and you understand your teacher's guidelines, the next step in research is to brain doodle—let your imagination play!

Suppose your topic is about outer space. You look into the sky one night and see a beautiful full moon. You become fascinated by the idea of walking around up there. Later, your mom tells you that when she was your age, she watched on TV as Neil Armstrong, an astronaut, become the first man to walk on the moon. You want to do your research about that, but you don't know where to start.

Go to the library and look up an article about that event. Many magazines had wonderful articles with lots of great pictures about Armstrong's walk on the moon. Read one or two articles. Think about what it was like. Picture it in your mind. Ask yourself what interests you most about this story, and write down your ideas and questions. Your project could take many different directions. Here are a few:

What did Armstrong see and feel as the first man on the moon?
How was Armstrong trained as an astronaut?
How was Armstrong selected to be the first astronaut to walk on the moon?
How did his "moonwalk" affect the rest of Armstrong's life?
What did scientists learn from Armstrong's experience?
Did Armstrong bring anything, such as rocks, from the moon for scientists to study?

For another example, let's say that you are fascinated with dinosaurs and you want to learn more about them. Look up dinosaurs in *The World Book Encyclopedia*. (That encyclopedia, by the way, has a very good list of questions about most topics. Those questions can be good material for brain doodling.) As you read, let your brain play. Draw your brain doodles in pictures if you like. Here's how that might look:

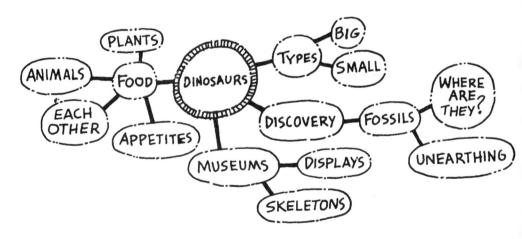

Let's take one more example and do some extensive brain doodling. Imagine that your math teacher mentions that she has a part-time job after school. A curious student asks, "Doing what, Ms. Lyon?" Your math teacher confesses—she's a part-time lion trainer! You decide this would make a great topic for a report, and your language arts teacher approves the idea. This report should be lots of fun.

How do you begin? You start by brain doodling—thinking up ideas and questions about the topic.

Think of some questions you have about this topic

Write them down on separate pieces of paper or, even better, on 3×5 or 4×6 note cards. (We'll talk more about taking notes in Chapter Five.)

> How did she get interested in training lions?
> What do my math teacher's family and friends think about her part-time job?
> Does she like lion training more than teaching math? How are her two jobs different?

Read an encyclopedia article on lion training in your school library

Let your imagination run wild, and write whatever questions come to your mind. (In Chapter Two we'll talk more about how to find what you're looking for in the library.)

> Who is the most famous lion trainer of all time?
> How often do lion trainers get hurt?
> Has my teacher ever gotten hurt by a lion?
> What other types of trained animals are there in circuses and shows?

Talk to someone who knows the topic well

Talk to your math teacher for a few minutes about your project. Whenever she says something that gives you an interesting idea or question, write it down. (In Chapter Four we'll talk more about how to do interviews.)

> Where does my math teacher work as a lion trainer?
> Does she like both her jobs?

> Where did my math teacher grow up?
> What kinds of sports do math teachers like?

Read a magazine or newspaper article about lion training

Maybe your math teacher will lend you one. If she doesn't have any, your librarian can help. As you read, write down interesting ideas or questions.

> How long does it take to become a lion trainer?
> What are their secrets with the lions?
> How many trained lions are there in this country?

There are many ways you can come up with a list of interesting questions about your topic: books, magazine articles, newspaper articles, Internet sites, movies, videos, encyclopedias, conversations with experts, and many more. Pick whatever ways you like.

Brain doodle until you have several interesting ideas or questions about the topic in your mind. Your ideas and your questions about the topic are very important. They are the key ingredients in the next step of research—making a good search plan.

Making a plan for your search

Imagine that you hear someone say there's buried treasure near your home. You believe there is some kind of treasure to be found, but you have no idea where to look. Would you just grab a shovel and start digging? You could waste a lot of time digging all over town—backyards, city parks, even the garbage dump. You surely could use a treasure map! A map would save you lots of time and frustration because it would tell you exactly where to dig. In research, having a good plan is just like having a treasure map.

Let's take the example of Ms. Lyon's part-time job. Having a good plan helps you avoid trying to answer a zillion questions that don't need to be answered. If you go straight to the library, pull down books on math teachers and lions, and start taking notes on everything you read, you will soon have information about lions' habitats in the wild, their diets, how they care for their young, how math teachers are trained in college, and all sorts of things that may not be related to your topic. It's just like going on a treasure hunt without a map.

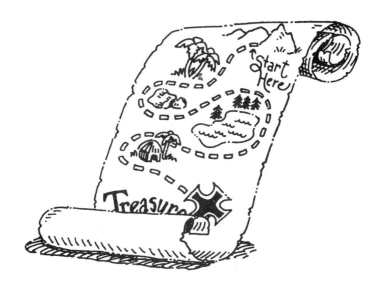

How can you use those 14 questions about Ms. Lyon to create a good research plan—one that will tell you exactly what information to look for? Your first task is to sort those 14 questions into groups.

Look over the 14 questions again and again until you begin to see how they fall into groups of key ideas. There are many ways you could organize your questions into groups, so shuffle them up a few times and see if you like the groupings better. Here's an example of what the first key idea in this paper might be and the questions that fit that key idea:

KEY IDEA A: ABOUT MY MATH TEACHER
Where did my math teacher grow up?
Where does my math teacher work as a lion trainer?
How did she get interested in lion training?
What do my math teacher's family and friends think about her part-time job?

Let's organize the rest of the 14 questions into key ideas. Keep in mind that each question should fit with the others in its group and describe the key idea.

KEY IDEA B: ABOUT LION TRAINING AND LION TRAINERS

Who is the most famous lion trainer of all time?

How long does it take to become a lion trainer?

KEY IDEA C: DANGERS OF THE JOB

Has my teacher ever gotten hurt by a lion?

How often do lion trainers get hurt?

KEY IDEA D: WHAT IS THE LION TRAINER'S MAGIC TOUCH?

What are their secrets with the lions?

KEY IDEA E: MY TEACHER'S TWO DIFFERENT JOBS

Does she like both her jobs?

Does she like lion training more than teaching math?

How are her two jobs different?

LEFTOVER QUESTIONS THAT I DON'T KNOW WHERE TO PUT

1. How many trained lions are there in this country?
2. What other types of trained animals are there in circuses and shows?
3. What kinds of sports do math teachers like?

Let's take a close look at these leftover questions. The first question in this list fits well under Key Idea B. Let's put it in that stack.

The second question doesn't really have anything to do with Ms. Lyon and her part-time job. If you realize that some of your questions don't fit well, put them aside. You might use them later and you might end up throwing them out. Since we already have plenty of questions for this paper, let's throw out this one.

The third question is what we call a "say what?" question. It doesn't make much sense. This paper is about one math teacher who is a part-time lion trainer, so it isn't relevant whether other math teachers like football or Frisbee golf. Don't feel bad when you catch a few "say what?" questions in your list. In fact, if you don't find a few of them, you probably could have had more fun with your brain doodling. A few of your wild and crazy questions might turn into great projects someday.

You've done some very good work by asking interesting questions and organizing them into key ideas. Now your search plan is ready to use, and here are some ways it helps you:

- It gives you a crystal clear picture what your project is about.
- It tells you exactly what information to look for.
- It helps you see what types of information you don't need to look for.
- It helps you avoid confusion, frustration, and wasted time when you go to the library or log onto the Internet.

BRAIN TICKLERS
Set #3

1. Lillian's teacher says, "Write a three-page research report on anything in the world— or anything out of this world, for that matter." Lillian has always been fascinated by what happens to old newspapers when they get recycled. Her mom has a book about paper manufacturing and the library has one about recycled glass. She starts reading both books and taking lots of notes. Before long she is very frustrated and bored silly. What important step did Lillian skip?

2. Your research project is about different theories on why the dinosaurs became extinct. You did some reading and brain doodling, and you came up with ten interesting questions. Organize these ten questions into key ideas.

   (1) Was there an asteroid that hit the earth?
   (2) Was there a supernova explosion?
   (3) What is a supernova explosion and how would it kill the dinosaurs?
   (4) Did the earth become too cold?
   (5) How would an asteroid have killed the dinosaurs?
   (6) Did an increase in the number of mammals have an effect on the dinosaurs?
   (7) How long ago do some scientists think the asteroid hit?
   (8) What are the most recent findings about the possibility of an asteroid?
   (9) What about parasites and diseases?
   (10) Did dinosaurs have any natural predators that could have caused their extinction?

(Answers on page 34.)

Making a schedule

When you have a big project, it is always a good idea to make a list of things to do and a schedule of when to do them. Get a calendar and mark the day your research project is due. That's your final deadline. Now, count the number of days you have until the deadline. Let's imagine you have four weeks to do your project. This is usually a good breakdown for how much time the different parts of a project take:

WEEK 1:
   Decide on the topic of your project. Brain doodle and make your search plan.
WEEK 2:
   Do your research and take notes.
WEEK 3:
   Organize your note cards and write the first draft.
WEEK 4:
   Edit your paper and type the final copy.

Let's take a more complicated project. You are assigned to be part of a team of 10 kids who will prepare for your class a Thanksgiving feast just like the early settlers and Native American Indians shared. You will also write a short paper about the meaning of Thanksgiving. Sounds yummy but a little complicated. Let's see how you might break that one down into four weeks:

Week 1

- Think about what type of information you'll need (the history of early Thanksgiving celebrations and the types of food the settlers and Indians ate).
- Talk to your teacher about when the meal will be served (day and time), where it will be served (at school? indoors? outdoors?), how many people will be eating, and how the groceries will be paid for.
- Talk to all your team members about whose parents will be able to drive to the grocery store, help cook the meal, and help with the other necessary chores.
- If you're going to need costumes, talk to the adults about this early so they'll have time to help you.

Week 2

- Split up the research work. Have each student read a little bit about the early Thanksgiving celebrations.
- Take good notes, not only about the food they ate, but also about the meaning of Thanksgiving and the relationships between the Native American Indians and the settlers.

Week 3

- Organize the notes that all ten students took.
- Write the rough draft of your report on the history of Thanksgiving. You might all sit around together and write, or you might assign each student one specific idea or section of the paper.
- Make a grocery list of what food you'll need to buy. Go over the list with a parent or two to make sure you've done a good job estimating how much food to buy.

Week 4

- Write the final draft of your paper.
- Do the grocery shopping.
- Make sure you've arranged for plates, silverware, drinks, napkins, and all the things that are needed for a meal.
- Finish your costumes if you're going to wear any.
- Cook the meal and enjoy a Thanksgiving feast with your friends at school.

Imagine how stressed you ten kids would feel if you put all this work off until the last week! The Thanksgiving feast schedule might look long and complicated, but if you break it down into steps and have ten kids (and a few helpful adults) working on it, it's not so bad after all. All it takes is a little scheduling.

RESEARCH REPORTS VS. RESEARCH PAPERS

Research reports involve discovering and presenting information about a topic. Research papers (also called term papers or thesis papers) go a little deeper than reports. They involve making comparisons between two things, trying to prove that one idea is better than another idea, attempting to convince your reader that some previously believed theory is not true, or perhaps discussing the effects that one thing has on something else.

Reports are usually descriptions of a topic. Research papers make a specific point about the topic. They take a stand. That stand is called the thesis.

TOPIC:
what you're writing about

THESIS:
what you're trying to show or prove about the topic

TOPIC:
broccoli

THESIS:
Broccoli is a very healthful food.

TOPIC:
soccer

THESIS:
Soccer is as important in Europe as baseball is in the United States.

Here are some examples showing the difference between reports (about a topic) and research papers (about a thesis). Can you see how research papers go a little deeper than reports?

REPORT (TOPIC):
"Pollution in Our Hometown River"
(For this report, you would find information about pollution in the river that runs through your town, then tell your reader what you learned.)

RESEARCH PAPER (THESIS):

"Local Businesses Should Be Required to Clean Up Our Hometown River"

(For this paper, you would find background information about river pollution. You would go a little further and find out about arguments for and against mandatory cleanup. Then you would try to convince your readers that local businesses that dirty the river should be required to clean it up.)

RESEARCH PAPER (THESIS):

"Pollution in Our Hometown River: The Long-Term Effects on Our Health if We Don't Clean It Up"

(In this paper you would be making a link between two things—pollution and future health—showing how one effects or even causes the other.)

RESEARCH PAPER (THESIS):

"Three Different Plans for Cleaning Up the Pollution in Our Hometown River"

(In this paper, you would compare the strengths and weaknesses of three different clean-up plans that citizens in your town are considering.)

RESEARCH PAPER (THESIS):

"The 'Secret' Causes of Pollution in Our Hometown River"
(In this paper, you would be looking at why the river is polluted and particularly focusing on the causes that few people know about.)

Here are some more examples of the difference between a report (about a topic) and a research paper (about a thesis).

REPORT (TOPIC):

"The History of My Favorite Rock Group"

RESEARCH PAPER (THESIS):

"How the Music of My Favorite Rock Group Was Influenced by The Beatles and Bach"

RESEARCH PAPER (THESIS):

"Contributions My Favorite Rock Group Made to the Development of Popular Music in the 1990s"

REPORT (TOPIC):

"How Eagles Build Nests"

RESEARCH PAPER (THESIS):

"Eagle Nests Are Vulnerable to People and Should Be Protected by Law"

RESEARCH PAPER (THESIS):

"Eagle Nests Don't Need Protection Because They Are in Remote Locations"

In late middle school and especially high school, more of your assignments will be research papers. The key to success is to be very clear what your goal is. What is your thesis? What are you trying to prove? Being clear about your goal will keep you on track when you're researching and writing your paper.

BRAIN TICKLERS
Set #4

1. The assignment is to write a short research paper on the 1980 eruption of Mount St. Helens in the state of Washington. Sally does a report describing volcanoes. Where did Sally get off track?

2. John's teacher wants him to do a short research paper about sports heroes. He writes a report about Tiger Woods's most recent golf game. Where did John get off track?

3. The title of Evonda's research paper is "Why Abraham Lincoln Was Our Best President." What types of problems will Evonda encounter when she tries to support this thesis?

(Answers on page 35.)

BRAIN TICKLERS—
THE ANSWERS

Set #1, page 12

1. This topic is huge! It needs to be narrowed down unless the teacher wants a 10,000-page paper. Often one huge idea contains many fascinating smaller topics. If a student were interested in the life of Martin Luther King, Jr., imagine how many interesting topics there are to choose from. These are only a few:

   "The Childhood of Martin Luther King, Jr."

   "The Tragic Death of Martin Luther King, Jr."

   "What Martin Luther King, Jr. Taught America"

   "How Martin Luther King, Jr.'s Work Changed Life in Our City"

   "People in America Who Carry On Martin Luther King, Jr.'s Work"

2. Now that's a tiny topic. What about two-day-old Bengal tigers? What about their sleep habits, too? Here are a few ideas for making the topic of baby Bengal tigers bigger and better:

   "Baby Bengal Tigers Born in Captivity Compared to Those Born in the Wild"

   "How Mother Bengal Tigers Care for Their Young"

   "Effects of Pollution on the Health of Baby Bengal Tigers in the Wild"

3. The information you need for this paper probably won't be available in the school library since it happened so many years ago. If you don't mind going to the town library to look up old copies of the local newspaper, there's no problem here.

4. To find the information needed for this paper, a student would need to give questionnaires to all the teachers in the school or to interview them all personally. Gathering information through interviews and questionnaires is a fine way to do research, but it's important to remember that this would take a lot of time.

5. This paper will be very hard to research unless you enjoy reading very technical books and journals. If someone you know is a biologist and can help you locate and understand the technical information this paper will involve, then your job will be much easier. Otherwise, you'll be better off with a less complex topic.

6. Much too big! Here are some more manageable topics:

   "The Story of the Endangered American Crocodile"
   "Some Animals That Went from Endangered to Extinct"
   "Some Animals That Made It off the Endangered List and Are Increasing Their Population"
   "Types of Animals That Are Endangered in America Today"
   "Efforts in The United States to Save Endangered Animals"

Set #2, page 18

1. Hurricanes are not about winter weather. Hurricanes occur in summer and fall. They are tropical storms and need warm temperatures to grow. Here are three topics Allison could choose that would be on track with her teacher's guidelines:

   "Winter Storm Rescue Operations in the Rocky Mountains"
   "Snow Storms and Ice Storms: What's the Difference between Them?"
   "How Does a Snowflake Form?"

2. A seeing-eye dog helps a person adapt to physical problems, but its own body doesn't adapt in any particular way. Here are two on-track topics Sam could write about:

   "The Giraffe's Amazing Neck" (The giraffe can reach higher into the trees for food than any other animal, so it has less competition for food.)
   "The Camel's Amazing Hump" (The camel's hump contains fat, which serves as an energy reserve in extremely hot, dry climates where camels live.)

"The Elephant's Amazing Trunk" (Elephants have very heavy heads, so they needed to develop short, strong necks.)

Set #3, page 26

1. Lillian didn't brain doodle! By jumping straight into reading and note taking without asking herself some questions and making a search plan, Lillian got far off track from her topic. In this case she overlooked the fact that recycling glass and recycling newspapers are different processes. Also, manufacturing of paper covers a lot of territory, and much of that territory has nothing to do with recycling. Lillian did a lot of reading, but she didn't find the answers she was interested in, and she ended up frustrated as a result.

   If you know a lot about your topic, you can start by asking specific questions that interest you. (Where are the newspapers taken? What are they turned into? How does that happen? How much does that cost?) If you don't know a lot about your topic, go to the library and read one or two magazine articles about it or look it up in an encyclopedia.

Learn a little about your topic so you know what questions interest you.

Play with the idea, ask lots of questions, and organize those questions into key ideas. Those questions are your guides; they tell you exactly what to look for when you begin your research.

2. There are many ways to organize questions into key ideas. Just be sure that all the questions under a key idea make sense together.

Key Idea A: The asteroid theory
   (1) Was there an asteroid that hit the earth?
   (5) How would an asteroid have killed the dinosaurs?
   (7) How long ago do scientists think the asteroid hit?
   (8) What are the most recent findings about the possibility of an asteroid?

Key Idea B: The supernova theory
   (2) Was there a supernova explosion?
   (3) What is a supernova explosion and how would it kill the dinosaurs?

Key Idea C: Other theories
   (4) Did the earth become too cold?
   (6) Did an increase in the number of mammals have an effect on the dinosaurs?
   (9) What about parasites and diseases?
   (10) Did34 dinosaurs have any natural predators that could have caused their extinction?

Set #4, page 31

1. Sally forgot that a term paper goes deeper than a report. A report on volcanoes might be very interesting, but it is not a research paper. For a research paper, Sally needs a thesis—a comparison she's making, a point she's trying to prove, or something she's trying to convince her reader of. Here are some possible theses:

   "The Efforts to Prevent Deaths at Mount St. Helens Were Heroic and Effective"

"The Efforts to Prevent Deaths at Mount St. Helens Were Weak and Ineffective"

"A Comparison Between the 1980 Eruption of Mount St. Helens and the Eruption of Mount Vesuvius in 79 A.D."

2. There are two problems here. First, heroes is plural. John needs to write about two or more sports heroes. Second, the teacher asked for a research paper. A description of Tiger Woods's most recent golf game does not have a thesis. Here are some possible theses John could write about:

"A Comparison of Playing Styles of Tiger Woods and Lee Trevino"

"Why Soccer Players Make Good Heroes for Kids"

"A Comparison of Social and Charitable Works of Michael Jordan and Arthur Ashe"

3. The topic of this paper is Abraham Lincoln. The thesis (what Evonda is trying to prove) is that he was the best president we ever had. That's a great project if Evonda has about five years to do the research and about five tons of paper in her computer printer. The way she has stated the thesis, she is going to have to research every single president and compare Lincoln with each of them. What a job! If her topic is Abraham Lincoln, these would be much easier (but still very interesting and challenging) theses:

"The Civil War Helped Abraham Lincoln Bring an End to Slavery"

"The Presidency of Abraham Lincoln Influenced American Politics for More than 100 Years"

"A Comparison of the Views Expressed by Abraham Lincoln and Stephen Douglas in the Debates of 1858"

CHAPTER TWO

Digging for the Treasure

Research is a search for treasure. It's like opening a lot of oysters to find a few awesome pearls or exploring the rain forest to find a type of monkey nobody knew existed. If you approach it right, doing your research won't be dull or boring at all; it will feel like you're on an exciting and fun adventure. After all, people have been doing research since they began writing things down about 5,500 years ago!

FINDING YOUR WAY
AROUND THE LIBRARY

You know your treasure is buried somewhere in the library, but where? To find it, you need to know your way around. Libraries are organized so that things are easy to find. If you are looking for a particular encyclopedia, for example, you go to the reference section. With a quick glance at the shelves you can usually find exactly what you need.

Every library or media center, including the one at your school, is divided into sections. Often, one big room of a library contains many sections. Here is a description of the sections you find in most libraries.

Reference

The reference section contains encyclopedias, maps, atlases, almanacs, indexes, yearbooks, directories, and more. Lots of information for your research project is probably available here. Since these books cannot be checked out and taken home, the reference section has desks where you can do your work.

The stacks

Usually the biggest part of a library, this is where you find books that may be checked out. The shelves in this section contain thousands, maybe tens of thousands, of books. There are two types of books in the stacks, fiction and nonfiction. Fiction books consist of stories that writers have made up. Nonfiction books contain factual material on subjects ranging from aardvarks to zucchini.

Periodicals

This section contains newspapers and magazines. These materials are called periodicals because they are published periodically—at the end of a specific period of time. A daily newspaper is published, obviously, every day. Many magazines are published monthly. Some are quarterly, which means they are published four times a year.

Non print

This section is where you find video tapes, CD-ROMs, music recordings, art prints, and other materials that are not printed in words.

Vertical files and artifacts (odds and ends)

You might find pictures or objects from foreign countries that teachers in your school have brought back from trips. You might find a collection of antique dolls or rare stamps someone donated to the library. You might find travel brochures or specialized catalogs. Each library has a very different collection of odds and ends. If you're curious whether your library might have something useful for your project, ask the librarian.

Caution! Major mistake territory!

When you start your research in the library it is easy to get overwhelmed by all the information available or to get sidetracked by interesting things you see along the way. Remember, research is like a search for a few rare trees in a thick forest. Even though you might see hundreds of different kinds of trees, you're looking for a few special ones. Don't stop to study every single tree along the way. Know what you're looking for and go after it!

A SMART START:
THE REFERENCE SECTION

A good spot to start digging for your treasure is the reference section of the library. Here's what you can find there:

General encyclopedias

This is where you begin many of your research projects. *The World Book Encyclopedia* is a general encyclopedia. So are *Academic American Encyclopedia, Collier's Encyclopedia, Encyclopedia Americana,* and *New Encyclopedia Brittanica.* General encyclopedias give information about a whole lot of topics, and it is easy to find what you're looking for.

Ask your teacher how many encyclopedias you may use for your project. Your teacher might say, for example, that you need four sources of information for your project, and only one may be an encyclopedia. This is to encourage you to find information in other places as well: books, magazines, newspapers, etc.

Specialized encyclopedias

These encyclopedias give much more in-depth information than general encyclopedias. There are specialized encyclopedias devoted to sports, science, medicine, dance, inventions, gardening, and many other subjects. Here are a few examples of specialized encyclopedias:

> *Encyclopedia of Western Lawmen and Outlaws*
> *Encyclopedia of Sports Talk*
> *Ebony Pictorial History of Black America*
> *Encyclopedia of Phobias, Fears and Anxieties*
> *How It Works: The Illustrated Encyclopedia of Science and Technology*
> *The Encyclopedia of Health and the Human Body*
> *The Illustrated Encyclopedia of the Animal Kingdom*
> *Macmillan Encyclopedia of Science*

Dictionaries

Dictionaries are books that define things. The most common types give definitions of English words, but there are many other types of dictionaries. There are dictionaries of culprits and criminals, historic nicknames, imaginary beings, and silverware, to name just a few.

Maps and atlases

Most libraries have a large collection of maps showing every place in the world—including the ocean bottoms and outer space. Atlases are books that present information in the form of maps. Some atlases are historical (*Atlas of the Crusades*, for example); others deal with specific topics (*Atlas of Cats of the World*, for example).

Yearbooks

If you want to know what happened in the world the year you were born, the best place to look is probably a yearbook. Yearbooks are sometimes printed as updates to encyclopedias. Other times they are reviews of the year's events in some specific area, such as *Halliwell's 1997 Film and Video Guide*.

Almanacs

Almanacs are published each year and contain a lot of statistics about many subjects. Do you want to know the most popular shows in television history, the population of every country in the world, or the score of every Super Bowl game ever played? Check an almanac.

Biographical references

If your project is about a particular person, this is a great place to look. These books give details about the lives of notable people. One of the best known is *Who's Who*. Another fact-filled publication is *Current Biography*. (These two references are about people who are still alive, so they wouldn't be much help if you're looking up information about George Washington.) There are many other biographical references about people living and dead. Here are a few examples:

Men and Women of Space
Biographical Dictionary of American Sports
Women Who Ruled
Rock Movers and Shakers: An A to Z of the People Who
  Made Rock Happen

Directories

These books give addresses and phone numbers of people, businesses, and organizations. If you want to write or call Nintendo to find out information about one of their games, look in a directory. Here are a few examples of directories:

Encyclopedia of Associations
National Directory of Addresses and Telephone Numbers

CD-ROM

This stands for Compact Disk—Read Only Memory. That means a computer can read information from the disk, but it can't copy anything onto the disk. If your library has computers, it may also have general encyclopedias or specialized encyclopedias on CD-ROM. Encyclopedias on CD-ROM are often referred to as "multimedia encyclopedias." That means they have picture and sound entries as well as text.

Your library may also have indexes on CD-ROM for various newspapers and magazines (we'll talk more about those later). Be sure to ask your librarian what is available to you on CD-ROM.

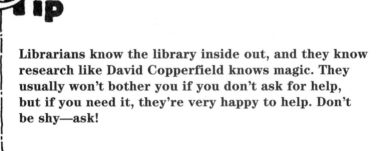

Tip

Librarians know the library inside out, and they know research like David Copperfield knows magic. They usually won't bother you if you don't ask for help, but if you need it, they're very happy to help. Don't be shy—ask!

Using the encyclopedia index

Imagine that Christmas is just around the corner and your part of the class holiday project is to research the history of Santa Claus and the giving of gifts. You go to *The World Book Encyclopedia*, pull down the S volume, and look up "Santa Claus." After you read what's there, you think you know everything *The World Book* has to say about Santa Claus. Oops—you forgot a very important step: checking the index. Look what we found in the index of *The 1997 World Book Encyclopedia*:

If you look only in volume S on page 113 under "Santa Claus," you would miss all the other information in volume C and volume N. You also would miss the information about the feast of Saint Nicholas in volume S on page 51. And you might never know that there is a town in Indiana named Santa Claus.

The index is usually found in the very last volume in an encyclopedia set. Always look up your topic in the index. Otherwise, you might miss some very helpful information.

Using specialized encyclopedias

Let's say your parents take you to a pet show. You see big dogs with short legs, fluffy kittens with pink ribbons in their fur, horses small enough to put in a cardboard box, and even a few tame boa constrictors. The animal that you fall in love with is an adorable shorthair cat with spotted fur that makes it look like a small leopard or ocelot. The owner tells you it's called an ocicat (pronounced ossy-cat).

The next day you go to the media center after school and look in every general encyclopedia you can find under "ocicat." Nothing. You look under "cat;" still nothing about ocicats. Do you think the owner told you the wrong name? Why can't you find any information?

First, ocicats are a very new breed. Second, there aren't many of them. Not many general encyclopedias have information about something so rare.

Don't despair. Research can be like looking for a four-leaf clover. Sometimes you have to look in several spots to find your prize. Check out the specialized encyclopedias in the reference section of the library. There are many specialized encyclopedias about animals, and there are several specifically about cats. Some of them will probably have the information you're looking for.

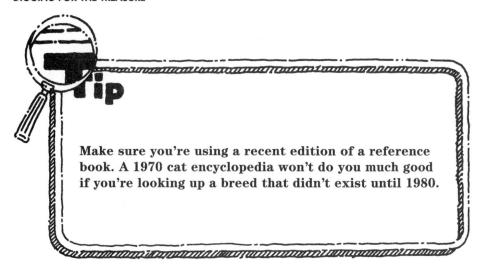

Tip

Make sure you're using a recent edition of a reference book. A 1970 cat encyclopedia won't do you much good if you're looking up a breed that didn't exist until 1980.

If your teacher has put a limit on how many encyclopedias you may use, ask if specialized encyclopedias count as encyclopedias or as books. Different teachers have different rules about this.

Reference materials are very good sources of information. But what if they don't have all the information you need or what if you need more than one or two sources for your project? Where's the next place to look? It's time to turn to books and magazines.

BOOKS AND MAGAZINES

Finding a book about your topic: card catalogs

Whatever your topic, your school library probably has two or three books that are packed with just the information you need. How are you going to find those books?

Fiction books are grouped together in the stacks. They are arranged in alphabetical order according to the last name of the author. If you wanted to find a copy of *Frankenstein*, a story by Mary Shelley, you would go to the shelf labeled "S" and look for Shelley.

If you wanted to find a copy of Peter Nye's *Hearts of Lions*, a nonfiction book about the history of bicycle racing, you would also find it in the stacks. But because this book contains factual information, it is kept in the nonfiction section. Books in this section are organized in a different way.

Each nonfiction book in the library has its own number (a "call number"), and books about similar topics are grouped together by number. This is called the Dewey Decimal Classification System. Devised by Melvil Dewey in 1876, this system has kept libraries from becoming big chaotic messes. Imagine that every time you wanted a book you had to dig through a pile of 10,000 books hoping to find just the one you were looking for. What a pain that would be! Thanks, Mr. Dewey.

This is how Dewey's system numbers the books in the library:

000–099	General works
100–199	Philosophy
200–299	Religion
300–399	Social sciences
400–499	Language
500–599	Pure science
600–699	Technology (applied science)
700–799	The arts
800–899	Literature
900–999	Geography and history

Knowing that certain kinds of books can be found together at a particular location can speed up your research. For example, let's say you are doing a project about photography and you want to browse through all the photography books that your library has. If you know that photography books have numbers in the 770s, you can go straight to the section on the arts (700–799), look for the 770s, and find books about photography.

Browsing the stacks can be a fun way to find what you're looking for, but it's not always the most efficient way. If you want to know what books the library has on your topic, you can check the library's catalog. Until a few years ago, every library had a card catalog (a bunch of drawers filled with small cards). Today, most libraries use computers for the job of listing all their books. Before long, there won't be many card catalogs left, but it's a good idea to know how to use one in case you are doing research at a library that hasn't put everything on computer yet. (Later in this chapter we'll talk about using computerized catalogs to find books in the library.)

You will find three kinds of cards in the card catalog:

Author card

These cards list each book by the last name of the author. If a book has more than one author, each author has his or her own card. If you know the name of the author (for example,

Rachel Carson or Stephen King), look up that name, then see if the library has the particular book you want. Here is a book about famous animals in movies written by Edward Edelson. You would find this card under the E's.

```
J 791.4    Edelson, Edward 1932–
Ede        Great animals of the movies

           Discusses the role of animals in films
           and profiles some of the more famous
           stars of the screen such as Lassie,
           Francis, the talking mule, Mr. Ed, and
           Cheetah. 1st ed.
           Garden City, N.Y. : Doubleday, c1980.

           134 p. : ill. ; 22 cm.
           includes index
```

Title card

These cards are listed according to the title of each book. If you know the title, this is an easy way to look up your book. Here's the same book, but this card is listed under the G's. Notice that the title is written at the top of the card.

```
           GREAT ANIMALS OF THE MOVIES
J 791.4    Edelson, Edward 1932–
Ede        Great animals of the movies

           Discusses the role of animals in films
           and profiles some of the more famous
           stars of the screen such as Lassie,
           Francis, the talking mule, Mr. Ed, and
           Cheetah. 1st ed.
           Garden City, N.Y. : Doubleday, c1980.

           134 p. : ill. ; 22 cm.
           includes index
```

Subject card

These cards group books together according to subject. Here is the same book again, but this card is listed under the A's and shows the subject at the top of the card.

ANIMALS IN MOTION PICTURES

J 791.4   Edelson, Edward 1932–
           Great animals of the movies

           Discusses the role of animals in films and profiles some of the more famous stars of the screen such as Lassie, Francis, the talking mule, Mr. Ed, and Cheetah. 1st ed.
           Garden City, N.Y. : Doubleday, c1980.

           134 p. : ill. ; 22 cm.
           includes index

When magazines and newspapers are good sources

If you are interested in a current event, magazines are often your best bet. It usually takes several years for a book to be published, but magazines come out every month or so, and there are magazines devoted to nearly every subject you can imagine.

Most magazines are written in an easy-to-read style. The articles are short and to the point, so it's often easy to find just what you're looking for. Imagine that your topic is "How John Smoltz Learned to Pitch." Books about baseball might have this information, but you're more likely to find it in a magazine interview with John Smoltz or an article in a sports magazine about how famous athletes got their starts.

One drawback about using magazines, however, is that the articles might not be as thorough as the information in books. Also, you might be getting only one point of view or only part of the story. A solution to these problems is to look up your topic in several different magazines, not just one.

With some topics, newspapers are your gold mine. Many newspapers come out daily, so the information is hot, fresh, and fast. If you want to know about the results of yesterday's election or the new solar system that was discovered last week, newspapers may be your best bet.

But because the information is hot and fast, it is also sometimes incomplete or wrong. Newspapers try to get a big story out before other newspapers even know about it. Even though they try their best to get all the facts correct, sometimes they goof. One of the most famous newspaper goofs occurred in 1948 when a Chicago newspaper incorrectly ran a front-page headline announcing that Thomas Dewey had won the presidential election the previous day when, in fact, Harry Truman had been re-elected.

If you are studying a current news event, check two or three different newspapers and read about the story over several days to see how it unfolds. That will ensure your getting as accurate and thorough a picture as possible.

Sometimes newspapers are also your best bet for information that is very old. If you want to know about the early history of your town and no books have been written about it, check old editions of your town's newspaper.

Using magazine and newspaper indexes

Several years ago, the only way to find articles in newspapers and magazines was to use indexes contained in big, fat books. When you found an article that looked good, you had to search the library to find the spot where that particular magazine was kept, then you had to look for the right volume. Now all that work can be done sitting in a comfortable chair in front of a computer screen.

Before we talk about the speedy, modern way to find newspaper and magazine articles with computers, let's talk about the old-fashioned way with indexes. Sometimes you won't be able to find everything you need on a computer database and you'll need to use an index.

There are many different indexes of magazine articles. The most common one is *The Reader's Guide to Periodical Literature*. You'll find it in the reference section of your school library or public library. This index lists articles from more than 150 popular magazines.

Let's imagine you are looking for information about ice fishing. You could start by looking in *The Reader's Guide* under "fishing," but we started by looking under "ice" and found this:

ICE FISHING
    Drill a bigger hole. W. Ryan. il *Outdoor Life* v194
    p57-9 D '94.
    Hard water made easy. J. Gibbs. il *Outdoor Life*
    v192 p48-51+ D '93

Two articles were listed, one by an author named W. Ryan and one by J. Gibbs. Both of these articles appear in the magazine *Outdoor Life*. Here's what else we know about those articles:

- il = this article is illustrated
- v194 = this article is in the magazine's volume 194
- p57-9 = this article starts on page 57 and ends on page 59
- D '94 = this article was in the December 1994 issue of the magazine

If you want to look up either article, you need to know whether your library has back copies of *Outdoor Life* and where those copies are kept.

Newspaper indexes work very much like magazine indexes. You look up your topic by subject (last year's biggest hurricane, the most recent space shuttle mission, last week's Super Bowl game, etc.). Your middle school library might not have newspaper indexes, but your town library does. *The New York Times Index* lists all major articles that have appeared in that newspaper since 1913. It is updated every two weeks. The library might also have indexes for other major newspapers, such as *The Washington Post*, as well as an index for a newspaper in your city or region.

The librarian can show you a list of magazines and newspapers that are available in the library.

Reading old newspapers at the library

Do your parents ever ask you to help recycle newspapers? If so, you know how big and heavy a Sunday edition of the newspaper can be. Can you imagine what it would be like if your town's library had to store all those copies for 50 years plus newspapers from several big cities around the country? The library would create a huge sink hole in the middle of town just from the weight of the newspapers!

Fortunately, scientists came up with ways to store newspapers as small pictures on film. This is called microfiche or microfilm. Microfilm comes in a long strip, and microfiche is stored on individual pages often the size of note cards. If you want to read the old newspapers, you will need to use special machines called readers. Your librarian can show you how to use these machines.

BRAIN TICKLERS
Set #5

1. Let's say that you want to know about springer spaniels and the only place you are allowed to look is in the reference section at the library. No magazines, no newspapers, no books from the stacks— just the reference section. You look in a general encyclopedia under "springer" and there's nothing there. What could you do next?

2. You are studying anorexia among middle school female athletes. You want to check for magazine articles about the subject, so you ask your librarian to show you where to find *The Reader's Guide to Periodical Literature*. You pull down the 1995 edition and look up anorexia. This is what you find:

ANOREXIA NERVOSA
The A's and B's of eating disorders: eating to
    extremes [cover story] S. R. Arbetter. il
    Current Health 2 v21 p6-12 S '94
Eaten alive [T. Sweeney] J. Levine. il pors
    Sassy v8 p76-80 Ag '95
Her secret pain: Countess Spencer struggles
    with anorexia, alcoholism and a troubled
    marriage. M. Green. il pors *People Weekly*
    v43 p129-30 Ap 17 '95
Hitting her stride [struggle with bulimia and
    anorexia]; ed. by Margie Bonnett Sellinger.
    E.H. Pena. il pors *People Weekly* v43 p115-17+
    Ap 10 '95

"I was dying to be thin." S. Solin. il pors
    Seventeen v54 p124-9 N '95
My private hell; ed. by Laura Muha. L.-J.
    Bonarcore. il pors Redbook v184 p46+ Ja '95

Do any of these articles look useful to you? Where would you find the articles?

(Answers on page 77.)

USING THE COMPUTER

Computer, find me a book

A computerized catalog makes the job of searching for a book fast and easy. Different libraries use different computer software to organize their books, so the computer screen at one library might look different from the screen at another library. However, once you learn one system, it is very easy to learn others. All computerized catalogs are similar in many ways, and all of them give you the same type of information.

The best way to get familiar with the computer in your library is to experiment for a few minutes. Sit down at a computer and access the library's catalog. (If you don't know what commands to use, look around the computer station for instructions, ask someone else nearby who is using the catalog, or ask your librarian for help.) When you start, the screen might look something like this:

Browse by . . .   ❏ Contains
❏ Any word   ❏ Begins with
❏ Subject   ❏ Exact match
❏ Title   [   ]
❏ Author
❏ Call number   ❏ Detailed search
                         ❏ Browse

Or it might look something like this:

> You may search for library materials by any of the following:
>
> W>WORDS in titles, series, and content notes
> A>AUTHOR
> T>TITLE
> Y>AUTHOR/TITLE SEARCH
> S>SUBJECT
> C>CALL NO
>
> Choose one (W, A, T, Y, S, C)

Can you see how these two screens ask you similar questions and give you similar choices even though they look a little different? Both screens offer you a choice of searching for a book by the book's author, title, subject, call number, or a keyword.

Which way will you begin looking for books that you need for your project? A keyword search is a painless place to start.

Searching by keyword

In a keyword search you tell the computer to look for a word or a combination of words in the titles and notes of books in the library's computerized catalog. You can search using whatever word or words you want, so this is a quick and easy way to get going with your research.

Here's one way to use a keyword search. Let's say you recently went to a theme park and rode one of the fastest roller coasters in the country. Now you want to know more about who first got the idea for roller coasters and how the original ones were built. You begin your search for books in the library like this:

```
Browse by . . .          ❏ Contains
■ Any word               ❏ Begins with
❏ Subject                ■ Exact match
❏ Title        [roller coasters]
❏ Author
❏ Call number            ❏ Detailed search
                         ❏ Browse
```

You click on the box for "any word" (which is this computer's name for keyword), type in the words *roller coasters*, click the "exact match" box (we'll explain that a little later), and hit the enter key. The computer gives you a list of all the books in the library with the words *roller coasters* in the title or notes.

In our town library, this keyword search found only one book. It is called *Roller Coasters: An Illustrated Guide to the Rides in the United States and Canada* by Todd Throgmorton. This is how the entry for that book looks on the computer screen:

```
AUTHOR:    Throgmorton, Todd H., 1962–
TITLE:     Roller Coasters: an illustrated
           guide to the rides in the United
           States and Canada
IMPRINT:   Jefferson, N.C. : McFarland & Co.,
           c1993
DESCRIP:   v, 154 p. : ill.; 23 cm
NOTE:      includes index
SUBJECT:   Roller coasters—United States—
           Directories. Amusement Parks—
           United States—Directories. Roller
           coasters—History. Amusement
           rides.
Location:  main collection
                    Call no.: 791.0687 Thr
```

Does this look like a book you can use? Probably, but what if you want to read more books on the subject? Notice that this book is listed in the computerized catalog under four different subjects. Those subject headings are the key for finding more books about roller coasters.

Searching by subject

Go back to the search screen on the computer, click on the box for subject, type in the words *roller coasters*, hit the enter key, and this is what the computer might show you:

> You searched for the SUBJECT: roller coasters
> 3 SUBJECTS found, with 5 entries;
> SUBJECTS 1-3 are:
>
> 1 Roller Coasters Directories . . . . . 2 entries
> 2 Roller Coasters Fiction . . . . 1 entry
> 3 Roller Coasters History . . . . 2 entries

This library has five books on roller coasters, and two of them have a lot of information about roller coaster history. (One of those two books is the one by Throgmorton, but there's another book that the keyword search did not find because it did not have the words *roller coasters* in the title.) To see more about those two books on roller coaster history, you would type the number "3."

You can also do subject searches using the other subject words listed with the Throgmorton book, *amusement parks* and *amusement rides,* to find other books in the library on your topic.

Subject searches versus keyword searches

What's the difference between subject searches and keyword searches, and which one is better? A keyword search looks for one or more specific words in the title and notes about a book. These searches are very helpful in getting started, but they won't necessarily give you a list of all the books in the library about your topic. A subject search is more focused and finds all the books in the library listed under standardized subjects (that means that the subjects are the same from one library to the next). However, you have to know exactly the right subject words to tell the computer. Starting with a keyword search and then using subject searches can help you zero in on the target.

Here's another example of how using keyword searches and subject searches can help you find all the books the library has on your topic. You are interested in lost treasure. Let's start with a keyword search for "treasure." This is what the computer might show you:

You searched for the WORD: treasure
2 entries found, entries 1-2 are:

1. The atlas of shipwrecks & treasure
    Call # 910.4503 Pic   Date: 1994

2. Gold & silver, silver & gold
    Call # J 910.4 S   Date: 1988

Let's take a closer look at these two books. If we click on book number 1 or type the number "1," we see this:

AUTHOR: Pickford, Nigel
TITLE: The atlas of shipwrecks & treasure:
the history, location, and treasures
of ships lost at sea
EDITION: 1st American ed.
IMPRINT: London; New York: Dorling
Kindersley; Boston: Distributed
by Houghton Mifflin, 1994
DESCRIP: 1 atlas (200 p.): ill. (some col.),
col. maps; 32 cm.
NOTE: Includes bibliographical references
(p. 195) and index.
SUBJECT: Shipwrecks—Maps.
Buried treasure—Maps.
Shipwrecks.
Location: main collection
Call no.: 910.4503 Pic

If we click on book number 2 or type the number "2," we see this:

```
AUTHOR:    Schwartz, Alvin, 1927–
TITLE:     Gold & silver, silver & gold: tales
           of hidden treasure/ collected and
           retold by Alvin Schwartz; pictures
           by David Christiana
EDITION:   1st ed.
IMPRINT:   New York: Farrar, Straus, and
           Giroux, 1988
DESCRIP:   128 p.: ill.; 24 cm.
NOTE:      Includes bibliographical references
SUMMARY:   Presents legends, true stories,
           and tall tales about the hunting,
           finding, and losing of treasure,
           including pirate treasure and
           treasure not yet uncovered.
SUBJECT:   Buried treasure
Location:  juvenile collection
                        Call no.: J 910.4 S
```

Eureka! Not only are these books you can use, but they also show you some subject headings that may lead to more books about lost treasure. You now know you can use the words *shipwrecks* and *buried treasure* in subject searches to find a lot more books about lost treasure.

You can also go a step further. Notice the word *pirate* in the summary of the book by Alvin Schwartz. Try using that word in another keyword search and see what you come up with. Thinking creatively may help you find even more books about your topic.

But what about the question we started with—is a subject search better than a keyword search? That's like asking if chocolate ice cream is better than vanilla ice cream. Sometimes one is better, sometimes the other, and sometimes they are great mixed together. So go for it—mix your subject searches with your keyword searches. Do 'em both! That way you are less likely to miss anything the library has on your topic.

Searching by author

If you know the author of the book you're looking for, this is a very fast way to search. You might click on "author" or you might just type the author's name beside the author prompt. The prompt window might look something like this:

```
Browse by . . .              ❑ Contains
❑ Any word                   ❑ Begins with
❑ Subject                    ■ Exact match
❑ Title        ┌─────────────────┐
               │ Throgmorton     │
■ Author       └─────────────────┘
❑ Call number                ❑ Detailed search
                             ❑ Browse
```

Since we typed only the author's last name, we will get a list of all the books in the library written by people with the name Throgmorton. If we typed the author's full name, Todd Throgmorton, the computer would give us a list of only the books written by him (or anyone else with that exact name). Remember, though, that the list you get shows books that are available in *that* library. Todd Throgmorton might have written fifty other books, but if they aren't available in that particular library, they won't come up on the computer screen.

Searching by title

If you know the title of a book you want to find, click on the title button, then type the title. If you know only the first word of the title, no problem; the computer will find all books beginning with that word.

Computer, find me a magazine article or newspaper article

Articles from lots of different newspapers and magazines are available on CD-ROM databases. One popular database in middle schools and high schools is called SIRS, which stands for Social Issues Resource Series. Another is InfoTrac. Both SIRS and InfoTrac are collections of thousands of articles collected from different magazines and newspapers around the world. All those articles are stored right there on CD-ROM rather than in a big room of the library. That means you can search for an article, locate it, read it, and even print it out without ever leaving your chair.

Tip

If you're looking for a very current event, SIRS and InfoTrac on CD-ROM may not have what you need. Information services usually update their CD-ROMs several times a year; only online services are updated every day. If you need to find newspaper articles about last week's election, ask your librarian about Nexis or other online services that can lead you to the very latest news.

One super way to search for articles in these databases is by keyword. You remember that when you do a keyword search in a library catalog, the computer looks for the keyword only in book titles and notes. A keyword search in SIRS, InfoTrac, an encyclopedia on CD-ROM, the Internet, and many other databases looks through much more information than that. It searches every word of every article in the database (it does this job *incredibly fast*), tells you how many articles contain that keyword, and gives you a list of all those articles.

Sounds pretty easy, doesn't it? Sometimes it is, but it can also get a little confusing. For example, if you told the computer to do a search using the keyword "Lincoln," you would get a list of articles about President Abraham Lincoln, the city of Lincoln in Nebraska, Lincoln automobiles, and maybe even Lincoln sheep. On the list might also be an article about President Kennedy (including one comment he made about Abraham Lincoln), an article about horse racing (maybe a well-known jockey is named Lincoln), an article about pizza manufacturing (maybe there's a factory on Lincoln Street in some small town), and lots of other articles that have absolutely nothing to do with what you're interested in.

If you're searching a gigantic database (the Internet, for example), it's not unusual to get over 10,000 hits (responses) from a keyword search! Imagine how much time it would take to look through all those articles. Fortunately, there's an easy way to tame the keyword monster—Boolean searches.

Even though it sounds like something you might yell on Halloween, there's no reason to be scared of the word *Boolean* (pronounced boo-lee-an). It's just a very clever way to look for things in a computer database. Named for the English mathematician George Boole (1815–1864), it is a system of searching that uses these small but powerful words: AND, OR, and NOT.

Imagine that you are doing research on famous women inventors in America. Your school library has SIRS and your librarian shows you how to access the database. If you ask the computer to search for "inventor," you'll get articles about both men and women. Let's use the Boolean system to help narrow the search.

Keyword Search

inventor

■ And   ❏ Or   ❏ Not

woman

❏ And   ❏ Or   ❏ Not

This is how the screen might look if you told SIRS to find every article in the database that contains the words *inventor* AND *woman*. The list that comes back will be much shorter than if you searched just by *inventor*.

But you can narrow the search still more. You want only information about famous women inventors in America—not in Russia, France, or any other country. The computer can help you eliminate all the articles that make no mention of America.

Keyword Search

inventor

■ And   ❑ Or   ❑ Not

woman

■ And   ❑ Or   ❑ Not

America

This time the computer gives you an even shorter list of articles. You still have to carefully look over the list to find the best articles and eliminate ones that aren't on track, but the computer has done a great job of selecting the best ones for you to examine.

Do you see from the woman inventor example how the word AND makes your list smaller? It's like saying, "I want a prom dress that's pink AND lacy AND floor length AND strapless AND has a bow in the back." By including all those AND's in your description, you have been very specific about the type of prom dress you want and narrowed down your choices a great deal.

The word NOT also narrows down your search. You could also say you want a prom dress that is NOT red NOT blue NOT white NOT silk and NOT floor length. Those NOT's narrow your selection of a prom dress quite a bit.

Let's say you want to find articles about a sea creature called a skate, but you don't want to have to sort through a lot of hits about ice skating or roller skating. Here's how that search might look:

Keyword Search

skate

❑ And   ❑ Or   ■ Not

roller

❑ And   ❑ Or   ■ Not

ice

69

The word OR makes your search bigger. Let's see how that works. If you go to the grocery store looking for food made of sugar AND chocolate, you'll come home with lots of chocolate cake, chocolate ice cream, and chocolate candy bars. If you go to the store looking for food made of sugar OR chocolate, you'll come home with vanilla ice cream, chocolate cookies, sweetened iced tea, bread (yes, bread usually contains a bit of sugar), sugarless chocolate candies, and about 15 grocery baskets of other goodies. Do you see how OR makes your grocery list grow?

Let's say you are interested in information about two planets: Neptune and Pluto. You could ask for information on the whole solar system or on all the planets, but then you would have to go through a very long list to pick out the ones about Pluto and Neptune. It's simpler to tell the computer to do that work for you. This is what you might tell the computer:

Keyword Search

Pluto

❑ And ■ Or ❑ Not

Neptune

❑ And ❑ Or ❑ Not

The computer will give you a list of all the articles that contain the word *Pluto* plus all the articles that contain the word *Neptune*.

You can mix up AND, OR, and NOT almost any way you wish. Think about what you want to find, and usually there's a way to tell the computer to look for exactly that. Check this out:

You could tell the computer	If you wanted articles about
Baseball AND teenager AND boy	teenage boys playing baseball
Baseball AND boy NOT teenager	pre-teenage males playing baseball
Baseball AND teenager NOT boy	teenage girls playing baseball
Baseball AND teenager AND girl	teenage girls playing baseball
Baseball NOT teenager NOT boy	pre-teenage girls, adult women, and adult men playing baseball
Baseball OR teenager	everything about baseball PLUS everything about teenagers (This would be a very long list!)

Tip

When you get a list of articles on the screen, you can click a button to read a short summary of each article. Because it helps you decide which articles are worth reading, that little button saves you lots of time! You can select the three or four articles that look best, then read them on the computer screen or print them out to read later.

Troubleshooting computer search problems

If your search doesn't find any books or articles that look useful, here are some ideas for getting the computer to behave better:

Check your spelling

If you ask the computer to find articles on "sherrif," it will tell you there are no such articles (it will say something like "no matches found"). The computer doesn't know you meant to type the word *sheriff*.

Check hyphenation and spacing in words

If you don't find "rollerblading," look up "roller blading." If nothing shows up under "in line skating," try "in-line skating" and "inline skating."

Try singular or plural words

Sometimes computers see a huge difference between singular and plural words. If the computer doesn't find much under "whales," ask it to search for "whale." If it can't find any articles about "flies," ask it to look for "fly." The computer at one library we checked found only one book when we did a keyword search for "roller coaster" (and that book wasn't about the carnival ride) but found several when we typed "roller coasters."

Think of synonyms

If you are looking for a book on race cars, try looking under "car," "race," "automobile," and "racing." If you're looking for a book about the planet Jupiter, look under "Jupiter," "planets," "space," and "solar system." If you want information about ferris wheels, try "ferris wheel," "amusement parks," and "carnivals." Often a book or article will be listed under more than one subject.

Be aware of abbreviations and numerals

If you don't get many hits using "20th century," try "twentieth century." If your computer doesn't seem to know what you mean by "U.S.A.," try "U.S." or "US" or "USA" or "United States" or "America."

Experiment with keywords

If you're not sure whether it's *Jurassic Park* or *Jurrasic Park* you're looking for, try a keyword search for "park." You'll get a list that includes *Jurassic Park*, *The Amusement Park Mystery*, *Once More Around the Park: A Baseball Reader*, and every other book or article with the word *park* somewhere in the title or notes. (The search might also find books with the words *parking* or *parka* or *parks* in them as well as authors, publishers, illustrators, etc., named Park, Parker, or Parks.)

Use the shortcut buttons

When they might help you, click one of the shortcut buttons of "starts with," "contains," or "exact match." If you are searching for "cat" and select "starts with," you get information about <u>Cat</u>holicism, <u>cat</u>apults, <u>cat</u>astrophes, <u>cat</u>echism, <u>cat</u>erpillars, the book <u>*Cat*</u>*cher in the Rye*, and more. If you select "contains," you get information about de<u>cat</u>hlons, communi<u>cat</u>ions, publi<u>cat</u>ions, and more. If you select "exact match," you get information only about the animal and other things nicknamed "cat."

Check the alphabetization

Entries are arranged in alphabetical order in computers (and in card catalogs), but sometimes that order can be tricky. *Snow leopard* comes before *snow-blind*, and that comes before *snowball*. The words *a*, *an*, and *the* don't count, so you would find *A Tale of Two Cities* under the letter *T*. Numbers are listed alphabetically before letters, so the book *101 Questions and Answers about Zebras* comes before *Aardvarks of the World*.

BRAIN TICKLERS
Set #6

1. Let's say you want to look for more articles about anorexia among middle school female athletes. Your school library has SIRS (or some similar type of database) on CD-ROM. How would you look up information about your topic?

2. You're at the library and you want to find a book about training your new puppy. Your friend told you he recently read a great book called something like *Train Your Dog Naturally*, but he couldn't remember the exact title. You know if you ask the computer to search for *dog* you're going to get books about dog shows, breeds of dogs, and lots of other material that you don't want. You know if you type in the word *train* you're going to get *The Little Engine That Could* and lots of information on locomotives. What could you do?

3. You've done a keyword search for a library book on roller coasters and found the book by Todd Throgmorton. Can you tell what year this book was published and how many pages it has? Can you tell who published it? Does it have pictures or illustrations?

```
AUTHOR:    Throgmorton, Todd H., 1962–
TITLE:     Roller Coasters: an illustrated
           guide to the rides in the United
           States and Canada
IMPRINT:   Jefferson, N.C.: McFarland & Co.,
           c1993
DESCRIP:   v, 154 p.: ill.; 23 cm
NOTE:      includes index
SUBJECT:   Roller coasters—United States—
           Directories. Amusement Parks—
           United States—Directories.
           Roller coasters—History.
           Amusement rides.
Location:  main collection
                        Call no.: 791.0687 Thr
```

(Answers on page 78.)

OTHER WAYS TO LOCATE BOOKS ABOUT YOUR TOPIC

Let's imagine that you just learned that jellyfish are very ancient creatures. That bit of information piques your curiosity, and you want to know everything about them—how they eat, what they eat, how long they live, whether or not they are the things that sting you at the beach, and everything else you can find. You read a great magazine article that gives you some good information. The author of the article talks about a recently published book that she says is the best book ever written about jellyfish. You really want that book, but it's not in your school library. What do you do?

Go to nearby libraries

Call or go to the town library, other school libraries, or a nearby college library. See if they have the book.

Do a computer search for the book

Your library might have a computer link-up with other school libraries, town libraries, or even libraries in distant cities. Ask the librarian. If there is a link-up, you can check whether another library has the book without ever leaving your chair in your school media center. See whether you can get that book through an interlibrary loan.

Order the book

Look for the book in the publication *Books in Print*. You can find this book in your school library, any public library, most book stores, or on the Internet. It lists all books that are in print; in other words, every book that you could order through a bookstore. *Books in Print* is huge. It lists books three different ways. You can look up books by subject (jellyfish), title *(Jellyfish Are Not Just for Breakfast)*, or author (Fische, Jill E.). With your parents' permission, you can order the book through a local bookstore. If you sweet talk your school librarian or town librarian, they might even order the book for the library. After all, the books they want to buy are the books people like you want to read!

BRAIN TICKLERS— THE ANSWERS

Set #5, page 57

1. First of all, don't get discouraged. Just because you dig in one spot and don't find treasure, don't assume there's no treasure around. In this case, there are many things you can do.

   - Look in the same encyclopedia under "spaniel."
   - Look in the same encyclopedia under "dogs."
   - Look in the encyclopedia's index under "springer," "spaniel," and "dogs" to see if information about springer spaniels might be under some topic you hadn't thought of—maybe "pets."
   - Look in another encyclopedia or two. Often one encyclopedia will have information that another doesn't have.
   - Find the bookshelf in the reference section that has all the specialized encyclopedias. Look for ones about animals, nature, dogs, or pets. Look in those under "springer" and "spaniel." You often find more in-depth information in specialized encyclopedias than in general encyclopedias.
   - Look around at the other shelves in the reference section. Do you see a dictionary about dogs? A picture guide to pets? Anything that might have information about springer spaniels?
   - If you run out of ideas, ask your librarian for help.

2. It's hard to tell from the titles whether any of these articles are specifically about anorexia among middle school female athletes. When you use a CD-ROM, you can often click a button and get a summary of each article, but you can't do that with *The Reader's Guide*. Several of these articles might have some useful information about the topic. Let's look at the information given in three of the entries:

- Her secret pain: Countess Spencer struggles with anorexia, alcoholism and a troubled marriage. M. Green. il pors *People Weekly* v43 p129-30 Ap 17 '95

This article is about an English countess. She's definitely not a middle school student and there's no indication from the title that this has anything to do with sports. The article is by M. Green. It was published in *People*. It appeared in the April 17, 1995, edition and is on page 129.

- Hitting her stride [struggle with bulimia and anorexia]; ed. by Margie Bonnett Sellinger. E.H. Pena. il pors *People Weekly* v43 p115-17+ Ap 10 '95

This article is also in *People* magazine. It sounds like this one might be about sports. To find it, you'd have to ask where *People* is kept in the library, then look for the April 10, 1995, edition. The article is on page 115.

- "I was dying to be thin." S. Solin. il pors *Seventeen* v54 p124-9 N '95

This article is in *Seventeen* magazine. Because of the types of stories *Seventeen* publishes, this might well be about a teenage girl, but we can't tell whether it has anything to do with sports. It was written by an author named S. Solin. It is in the November, 1995, edition on page 124. If your library has *Seventeen* back to 1995, you'll be able to find this article.

Set #6, page 74

1. We went to a middle school library and told SIRS to look up "anorexia." It came back with 60 articles. That was too many. We tried many different Boolean searches. (Each search, by the way, took about 10 seconds. What a speedy computer!) Here's what we found:

Search by	How many articles the computer found
Anorexia	60
Anorexia OR eating disorder	77
(Notice that OR makes the search bigger.)	
Anorexia AND sports	18
(Notice that AND makes the search smaller.)	
Anorexia NOT male	36
(Notice that NOT makes the search smaller.)	
Anorexia OR eating disorder AND sports	18
Anorexia AND middle school	0
Anorexia AND junior high school	3
Anorexia AND high school AND sports	6
Anorexia OR bulimia AND sports	20

What other words might we have used for searches? Maybe "teens" or "teenagers." Maybe "weight." Since we got a lot of hits on these searches, we stopped with these.

This isn't as many articles as you might think. There's a lot of overlap in these lists. For example, we discovered that the 18 articles under "anorexia AND sports" are exactly the same as the 18 under "anorexia OR eating disorder AND sports." But notice that the search "anorexia OR bulimia AND sports" picked up two additional articles.

When you do a search like this, read the summaries and see which articles look best. When you find the ones that look best, read the articles on the computer screen or print them out to take home and read later.

By the way, did you notice that in our search the computer found no articles about "anorexia AND middle school" but did find three articles about "anorexia AND junior high school"? Most likely the authors of the articles used the phrase "junior high school" and never mentioned "middle school." When you're doing research and you tell a computer what to do, you have to think creatively. But that makes sense—a computer is just a hunk of hardware; you're the one with the brain.

2. There are several ways you could search the library's computerized catalog. Let's start with a keyword search. A keyword search looks for specific words in the title and

in the notes (a description of the book that the librarian typed into the computer). A keyword search usually lets you type in more than one word. The prompt screen might look like this:

> WORD: | dog and train |
>
> Type in words from the title
>
> . . . then press the RETURN key

After we typed in "dog and train" and pressed the return key, here's what the computer at our town library showed us:

> You searched for the WORD: dog and train
> 4 ENTRIES found
>
> 1 The dog that took the train
> 2 The golden ball and other stories
> 3 The mentally sound dog: how to shape, train, and change canine behavior
> 4 Mother knows best: the natural way to train your dog

Book 1, book 3, and book 4 have words *dog* and *train* in the titles. Book 2 doesn't, but it must have those words in the notes. Book 4 looks like it might be the very book your friend recommended.

Now let's try a subject search. Remember that subjects are standard categories. If you don't know the correct category name, guess. We guessed "dog training." The computer said "Your SUBJECT not found, Nearby SUBJECTS are:" and then gave us a list of all the dog subjects. There's a subject called "dogs adoption," one called "dogs breeding," and one called "dogs cleaning." Farther down the list there's "dogs food" and even "dogs food recipes." Way down the list comes "dogs training." And there are 49 entries listed! Our town library has 49 books about dog training, not just the four we found when we did the keyword search.

First of all, why did the computer say our subject was not found? Because we typed "dog training." If we had typed "dogs training," the computer would have been happy. Silly computer. It didn't give us exactly what we wanted the first time, but it did a good job of leading us to the right territory.

And why did we get 49 books on dog training when we did a subject search and only four books when we did a keyword search for "dog and train"? Because the keyword search looks for specific words in titles and notes. Many of the books on dog training don't have both words—*dog* and *train*—in the title or notes. Here are a few examples:

Communicating with Your Dog
Dogs for Dummies
A Guide Dog Puppy Grows Up
How to Housebreak Your Dog in 7 Days

Keyword searches are quick and easy, and they allow you to use your own words; subject searches are more precise and thorough, but you have to know (or figure out) just the right words to use.

Does it seem confusing? Don't worry, just search. The more you practice searching, the simpler it all becomes. There are only a certain number of books about dog training in the library, and if you snoop around in the computer for a little while, you'll find them.

3.

```
AUTHOR:     Throgmorton, Todd H., 1962–
TITLE:      Roller Coasters: an illustrated
            guide to the rides in the United
            States and Canada
IMPRINT:    Jefferson, N.C.: McFarland & Co.,
            c1993
DESCRIP:    v, 154 p.: ill.; 23 cm
NOTE:       includes index
SUBJECT:    Roller coasters—United States—
            Directories. Amusement Parks—
            United States—Directories.
            Roller coasters—History.
            Amusement rides.
Location:   main collection
                        Call no.: 791.0687 Thr
```

What does all this information mean?

- 1962–: The author was born in 1962 and is still alive.
- Jefferson, N.C.: The book was published in the city of Jefferson, N.C.
- McFarland & Co.: This is the name of the company that published the book.
- c 1993: The "c" stands for copyright. This book was published in 1993.
- v: The book has a 5-page introduction (v is the Latin numeral for 5).
- 154 p.: The book is 154 pages long.
- ill.: This book is illustrated.
- 23 cm: The book is 23 centimeters tall.
- main collection: The book is in the library's main collection, not on a bookmobile or in a special section of the library (the children's room, for example).

CHAPTER THREE

The Internet

Can you believe it? When your parents were in middle school, nobody had computers in their homes or schools or libraries. It's not that your parents are *that* ancient, it's that computers are still very young. As technology goes, the Internet is still a baby.

But what a big baby it is! The Internet is one of the most fascinating and amazing things to happen in human history. For the first time ever, we have information from around the world, even from outer space, literally at our fingertips.

WHAT IS CYBERSPACE?

The year was 1969. Computers were becoming powerful enough to communicate with other computers, as well as solve problems assigned by some unbelievably tough math teachers. People in the U.S. Department of Defense decided it would be a good idea if several computers in different cities could be linked together so that when researchers solved a problem with one computer, they could share the answer with researchers who were using other computers. This would be a big help for all the people working on the same scientific project at different locations.

The first link-up was done with just four computer sites. That planted the seed. During the 1970s and 1980s, advances in technology allowed a greater number of computers to communicate with one another at faster and faster speeds. During the 1990s, the number of link-ups grew faster than Jack's beanstalk. Today there are hundreds of thousands (perhaps millions, nobody is sure) of computers all over the world linked together to form the Internet, also called the Net. You will also hear it referred to as Cyberspace, a word coined by the science fiction writer William Gibson to describe the "universe" created from this network of computers.

Any time you link different computers together so that they can talk to each other, you create a network. (Did you notice what the words NETwork and InterNET have in common?) The Internet is actually a huge network that links many smaller networks of computers. Special computers, called hosts, operate at very high speeds and link all the smaller networks. If you were to draw a diagram of the links among the host computers it might look something like a giant fish net covering the earth.

When the computer that you use at school or at home talks to the host computers on the Internet, it uses a modem. This is a device that takes what one computer says (digital speech) and turns it into an odd-sounding assortment of beeps and squeals (analog sounds) that go out over telephone lines. At the other end of the line, another modem turns these sounds back into digital speech that the computer on the receiving end understands.

WHAT IN THE WORLD IS THE WORLD WIDE WEB?

The Internet has many functions. One of the things that users of the first computer network found they liked most was the ability to exchange messages very quickly. Today you can send email to a friend on the other side of the world, and it'll get to your friend's computer in a matter of seconds. Other popular parts of the Internet are news groups (which are like long, running conversations of people who are interested in specific topics) and MUDs (which stands for Multiple User Dimensions). MUDs are games that many people can play at the same time on the Internet.

The part of the Internet that you are most likely to use for your research project is the World Wide Web. The Web is made up of millions of pages stored on computers around the world. While text information is common to the entire Internet, Web pages also give you sounds and pictures—sometimes motion pictures. You'll sometimes hear all that referred to as multimedia. If you looked up information on Ella Fitzgerald, for example, you would likely find written information about this famous African American singer, pictures of her, a recording of her singing voice, and maybe even a short movie or news clip of one of her performances.

Web pages are written in a special programming language called *html* (which stands for hypertext markup language). Hypertext links let you jump from one page to another just by clicking with your mouse on highlighted words or pictures. One Web page could contain links to hundreds of other pages, each of those with links to hundreds of other pages, each of those with links to hundreds more . . . on and on.

That's one way to explain how the World Wide Web works. If that sounds a bit too technical, here's another way to think about it. Imagine that all the books in a gigantic library came apart and the pages began to float, filling all the rooms from floor to ceiling with millions of pieces of paper. What a mess! If that happened you wouldn't be able to find the information you were looking for. Or would you? What if you had a special machine with a very long arm that could travel throughout the library and bring back exactly the page you wanted? What if that page were tied with very thin string to dozens of other pages with similar information that would be helpful for your research? And what if your special machine could collect all of those pages and deliver them in a neat pile on your desk?

That is how the Web works. When hooked by modem into the Web, your computer has virtual arms that stretch through telephone lines, travel all over the world, and bring back information on just about any topic you want.

Surf or go direct?

It's important to know that not everything you read on the Internet is true. When you go to the library and pull down a book to read, you can be pretty sure that it has been checked (many times) by editors not only for factual errors, but for spelling and grammar errors too. The same goes for most magazines and newspapers. That's not always true for the Internet.

Almost anybody can post a message in a news group or set up a homepage about anything they want. If we wanted, we could set up a Web page devoted entirely to strep throat problems among elephants that live in Alaska, even if there aren't any elephants in Alaska and regardless of whether they get strep throat. Since some people put information on the

Internet that is untrue, your best bet is to go to a reputable Web site. These sites are maintained by places like museums, colleges, libraries, businesses, and some private organizations. We reviewed hundreds of kid-friendly Internet sites and collected a list of the very best, covering just about every topic you could need for a project. That list is in Appendix C on page 233.

It's very tempting to "surf" the Web, clicking one link after another to see where you end up. Occasionally you stumble upon a good research site (a collection of pages), but usually you just waste a lot of time. The Internet is massive and it is not as well organized as a library. (Maybe someday it will be.) If you want to save time and get super information, don't surf. Go directly to reliable addresses.

Caution! Major mistake territory!

NEVER give out information about yourself before you've checked with a librarian, teacher, or parent. Sending a message that says you are a middle school student looking for information about a topic might be okay if you send it to the Smithsonian Institution or the Library of Congress, for example. It's not okay if you send it to a site owned by some person or organization that you are not sure of. Be safe. Ask your librarian, teacher, or parent before sending out any personal information about yourself.

The Web's crazy way of writing addresses

There are millions of individual pages on the World Wide Web and each one has its own address. One of the first things you'll get used to when you start working on the Web is the wacky way these addresses are written. Take a quick look on page 233. Notice that the addresses for pages on the Web begin with the letters *http*. This stands for hypertext transfer protocol, which is the system that lets you use hypertext links to jump quickly and easily from a page on one computer (perhaps in Chicago) to a page on a different computer (perhaps in Paris). You'll see lots of other weird-looking symbols and funny-sounding abbreviations, but don't worry; after a while you'll know them like your own telephone number and zip code.

Each of the symbols used in Internet addresses is a key on your computer. Sometimes symbols are on uppercase keys, such as the @ (at) key. You get that symbol by typing an uppercase version of the number 2. You see the @ symbol especially in email addresses, such as Bugs_Bunny@peskywabbit.org. This address is make believe, but the underline mark between *Bugs* and *Bunny* is really used in some email addresses. The underline (_) key is the uppercase dash (-) key.

Two symbols you often see in email messages are less than (<) and greater than (>). These are located on the comma key and on the period key. Anything that appears between these symbols is something that was written in a previous email message and is being repeated in the one you're reading.

There are a few other symbols you're likely to see in Internet addresses that are not often used when typing papers. The back slash (/) key is the lowercase question mark (?) key. The tilde key (~) is the uppercase accent (`) key, which is located at the upper left corner of the keyboard. The pipe (|) key is the upper case forward slash (\) key and is located below the delete key.

No matter what squiggly symbols you see in an Internet address, your computer is up to the task. Just look around on the keyboard until you find the right key.

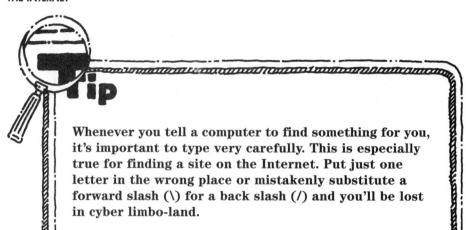

Whenever you tell a computer to find something for you, it's important to type very carefully. This is especially true for finding a site on the Internet. Put just one letter in the wrong place or mistakenly substitute a forward slash (\) for a back slash (/) and you'll be lost in cyber limbo-land.

Taking notes and saving pages from the Internet

Imagine that you've searched several pages on the World Wide Web and finally found one that has information you can use for your project. Now what? If this were an encyclopedia, you would take out your 3×5 note cards and begin taking notes. Guess what? That low-tech method works great with Web pages, too. Simply take notes on what you're reading.

Sometimes that may not be practical for two reasons: Time online costs money and other people may be waiting to use the computer. Fortunately, there are several ways to hold Web pages so you can take notes from them later. If you are working in your school library, your librarian can show you how to save pages in any of these ways:

- **Bookmark the page.** This is a way of telling your computer to remember the location of a page by copying its address into the computer's memory.
- **Copy the entire page** to the computer's memory.
- **Print out the page.** Be sure the printout includes the address of the page.

Tip

Whether you take notes now or later, be sure to copy the address of a page *exactly* as it appears on the computer screen. You'll need this address for your bibliography. If you need to go back to this Web site for more information and you forgot to write down the address, trying to find it again can be like trying to find one particular grain of sand on a big beach.

BRAIN TICKLERS
Set #7

1. Jonathan is new to Internet research. He needs some information for his project about waterfalls. His teacher told him there's a Wide World Web site about waterfalls in the mountains of North Carolina, so he logs onto the Internet to find it. Along the way he finds some interesting information about rock climbing camps in the North Carolina mountains. That leads him to Web sites about mountain climbing. He clicks on a few more links, and before long he's at the top of Mt. Everest. What advice would you give Jonathan?

2. Lisa is doing a science research project on rocket propulsion. She finds a site on the Web called Big Billy Bob and Sweet Sue's Sooper Dooper Physics and Rocket Science Home Page. She begins to read and some of the information sounds interesting. Do you think she should believe what she reads?

3. Kate is getting a horse for her birthday. Wow! After she gets over her shock, she heads for the Internet to find out more information about quarterhorses. She finds several sites and homepages, and she sends off some email to a few sites asking questions. Several people reply with answers and information. One person writes that if she sends her phone number and address, she'll receive some free color photos of quarterhorses. What should Kate do?

4. You have origami on your mind and you want to find out more about this ancient Japanese craft of folding paper to create butterflies, flowers, kites, and other objects. You log onto the Internet and type in an address you copied from a reference book: http:/www.lib.utexas,edu/Exhibits/orgami. The computer says something like "that address doesn't exist." What is your first guess about what the problem might be?

BRAIN TICKLERS— THE ANSWERS

Set #7, page 92

1. Surfing the Internet often leads to confusion, and it almost always eats up a lot of time. If Jonathan has a deadline for his research project, he should probably stop surfing and go direct. If he knows the address of the site about waterfalls in the North Carolina mountains, he could go straight there. If he doesn't know the address, he could do a Boolean search (perhaps asking the computer to search for "waterfall" AND "North Carolina" AND "mountain"), or he could ask his teacher, parent, or librarian for help in finding the site.

2. Big Billy Bob and Sweet Sue might be the finest rocket scientists in the country, or they might have no more expertise than shooting off a few fireworks for a Fourth of July celebration. How is Lisa to know? If she got this address from a NASA site or a Smithsonian site, she can probably trust it. If she saw this site written up in a respectable science journal, she can probably trust it. If she found it listed on a good link site for middle school science research, she can probably trust it. Otherwise, it would be wise for Lisa to ask her science teacher to help her determine whether the site is worthwhile.

3. Kate should *not* send her address, phone number, or other personal information to anyone she doesn't know on the Internet. She wouldn't give that information to a stranger on the street, so she shouldn't do it on the Net without clearing it with a parent or teacher.

4. When you're typing Internet addresses and the computer says it can't find that site, a good first guess is that you mis-typed something.

In this case, you typed:
http:/www.lib.utexas,edu/Exhibits/orgami.

The correct address is:
http://www.lib.utexas.edu/Exhibits/origami.

There are three tiny goofs, but any one of those goofs will confuse the computer. Do you see all three goofs?

CHAPTER FOUR

Interviews and More

Books, newspapers, magazines, encyclopedias, and the Internet are packed with information, and often you won't need any more material for your project than you can find with these sources. But sometimes you have to talk to people in order to get your answers.

Interviews come in two basic forms, the personal interview (when you ask questions of one particular person) and the questionnaire or survey (when you ask many people the same set of questions). If you are doing research on your math teacher's part-time job as a lion trainer, you would want to talk to her directly, either in person or over the telephone, to get the information you need. That would be a personal interview, and that's where we begin.

PREPARING FOR A PERSONAL INTERVIEW

Preparing for a personal interview is just like getting ready to do research in the library or on the Internet in one key way: You need a very clear idea of what you're looking for. Your first step is to write down a list of questions that you plan to ask. Once you have a list of questions, you will feel a lot more confident about doing the interview.

If you're unsure what questions to ask, all it takes is a little thinking about your topic. Remember in Chapter One how we put together a list of things we wanted to know about the math teacher, Ms. Lyon? Preparing for an interview involves the same process. Brain doodle! Let your curiosity go wild. Get out a sheet of paper or some note cards and write down whatever questions come into your head. Here are some pointers for preparing good interview questions:

Ask specific, clear questions

If you ask vague or unclear questions, your interviewee won't understand what you're asking and won't be able to give you interesting, helpful answers.

VAGUE:
> Tell me about yourself.

SPECIFIC:
> Tell me how it feels to walk into a cage of lions.

VAGUE:
> Was your childhood nice?
> (What does "nice" mean?)

SPECIFIC:
> Where did you grow up? How many brothers and sisters do you have? Were your parents involved in circuses in any way?

Ask deep, meaty questions

Try to avoid lazy questions, ones that could be answered with a simple yes or no.

LAZY:
> Do you like training lions?

MEATY:
> What is your biggest pleasure in training lions?

LAZY:
> Are you scared of lions?

MEATY:
> Tell me a story or two about times you've been frightened, what you did, what the lions did, and what you learned from those experiences.

Avoid obvious questions or ones you should already know the answers to

OBVIOUS:
> Do you like animals?

BETTER:
> What do you think it was in your childhood that got you interested in such an uncommon and potentially dangerous hobby?

Don't ask your interviewee to do your research for you!

YOU SHOULD ALREADY KNOW:

> There was an article about you in the local newspaper. What did it say?

BETTER:

> I read the article about you in the local newspaper. It said that you donate a lot of time to animal protection causes. Tell me more about that.

YOU CAN RESEARCH YOURSELF:

> When did the Ringling Brothers start their circus business?

BETTER:

> Have you ever trained with or performed with Ringling Brothers Barnum and Bailey Circus?

Here are a few more tips for a successful interview:

Be on time

Imagine how your interview would go if the first thing you said was, "I don't like you very much." Being late to a scheduled interview is a lot like saying just that. If you cannot avoid being late, let the interviewee know, and give that person the option of rescheduling.

Have all the materials you need

You will need paper, at least two good pens or pencils, and maybe a tape recorder and blank tapes. You wouldn't want to show up for an interview and have to borrow paper and pens from your interviewee.

Take good notes

While your interviewee is speaking, take notes. If you have access to the equipment and your interviewee says it's okay, you may want to tape record the interview. If you do, be sure your tape recorder is in good working order with fresh batteries and a blank tape. Even if you tape the interview, it's a good idea to take written notes in case something goes wrong with the recorder.

Courtesy counts

When you first contact the interviewee, introduce yourself and explain what the interview is for. During the interview, ask your questions with interest and politeness. Afterwards, it's good form to send your interviewee a short thank-you note.

WRITING A QUESTIONNAIRE

If you want to know what your math teacher does in her spare time, you would set up an interview with her. But what if you want to know what *many* people do in their spare time? You could set up interviews with 25 people, or even 25,000 people (if you had everybody in the whole school to help you). Or you could make up a questionnaire, give it to everyone from whom you want answers, then analyze the answers you get.

Writing a questionnaire is similar to preparing questions for a personal interview, with one important exception. If you ask questions that require long written answers, you probably won't get many responses. So, ask your questions in ways that call for short answers. Better yet, try to write questions that ask for "yes" or "no" responses.

Imagine that your project is on kids' favorite hobbies, and you want to find out what other students in your school do when they are not studying. To get that information you could talk to every single student, but by the time you finished you'd probably be in college. A better way is with a written questionnaire that you distribute either to all your fellow students or to a selected group. This is called a survey, and people who do them professionally are sometimes called pollsters. Here's a sample questionnaire about the favorite hobbies of kids in your school.

SAMPLE QUESTIONNAIRE

Are you a boy or girl?   Boy _____   Girl _____

What is your age? _____

What grade are you in? _____

What is your favorite hobby? _____

How many hours a week do you spend on this hobby? _____

List up to three other hobbies and the amount of time you usually spend on each hobby per week.

	Hobby	Hours/week
1)	_____	_____
2)	_____	_____
3)	_____	_____

How do you get money for your hobbies? (choose more than one if needed)

Parents _____   Relatives _____

Job _____   Tooth fairy _____

Other _____

Briefly describe what you like about your hobbies.

_____

_____

_____

Here are some tips for writing a questionnaire:

Ask clear questions

Have several people read over your questionnaire ahead of time looking for vague or unclear questions. If your respondents (the people who answer your questionnaire) don't understand what you're asking, the information you get back won't be very helpful.

> UNCLEAR:
> Who is your favorite TV character?
> (Different people would have different definitions of "character." Does this include fictional people such as Batman in movies shown on television? Real people such as anchormen on news shows? Characters in sitcoms?)
> CLEAR:
> Who is your favorite television cartoon character?
> CLEAR:
> Who is your favorite character in a weekly television sitcom?

Give simple choices so you will get simple answers

Complex questions are hard for your respondents to answer clearly, and complex answers are hard for you to analyze.

> TOO COMPLEX:
> What do you think about kids and TV?
> (What are you asking? What I think about kids? What I think about TV? What I think about kids watching TV?)
> CLEAR AND SIMPLE CHOICE:
> Do you believe that middle school students watch too much television? Please circle one choice:
> They watch too much television.
> They watch too little television.
> They watch about the right amount of television.

Prepare a cover sheet telling people what the research project is about

For example: "This project is to find out if eighth-grade boys and eighth-grade girls prefer different television programs. You will be asked to fill out a short, simple questionnaire about how much time you spend watching various television programs. Thank you for your help in this project."

Know how you will distribute the questionnaire

Will your teacher allow you to give one to every kid in your class? Should you set up a table in the lunchroom? Are you going to ask a dozen friends to fill out your questionnaire? Don't forget also to figure out how to get the questionnaires back from your respondents.

Keep it simple

This type of research can eat up a lot of time. Companies that specialize in surveys have armies of employees and powerful computers to do all the work. If you're doing everything by yourself, keep your project simple.

BRAIN TICKLERS
Set #8

1. Maria sets up an interview with Ms. Lyon to get information about her part-time job as a lion trainer. Maria sits down with Ms. Lyon and says, "Well, just tell me whatever you want to about yourself and about lions and stuff like that." Do you think Maria is going to get interesting, helpful information from Ms. Lyon?

2. Tony is interviewing a local woman who recently wrote a bestselling book. Tony says, "I haven't read your book yet, so please tell me about it." What's wrong?

3. Roxanne is writing a short questionnaire to give to 25 or 30 middle school students about their diets. Here is one of the questions on her questionnaire: "How much do you like to eat sweets and do you let yourself eat too much?" What's wrong with that question and how could she make it better?

(Answers on page 111.)

OTHER PLACES TO DIG FOR TREASURE

You know that the library and the Internet are rich sources of material for almost any project, and that interviews and questionnaires are sometimes the best ways to get the information you want. Are these the *only* places to look for information? Not at all! Put on your thinking cap and imagine all the places you might find excellent material for your project. Here are some ideas:

- **The Chamber of Commerce** in your town has lots of information about your town: businesses, history, population, and more.

- **Local historical societies** often have artifacts such as old letters or diaries of important people in your town, photographs from the town's early years, and other information about your town's history. You probably won't be able to take any of these materials home, but a friendly call to the curator (that's the person in charge of the materials) might get you access to some really interesting information for your research.

- **Museums** are a great source of information. A local art museum, history museum, or historic site will have information about the types of things they show there. The curators can also help you locate information they don't have on hand.

- **Travel agents** often have information about states and countries. Every state has a tourist office that will send you free travel brochures and information about that state. Most countries will do the same. Ask your librarian how to look up their addresses.

- **Government agencies** have tons of information on everything imaginable from A (the Air and Space Museum) to Z (zinc mining in the United States). The librarian can show you how to find lists of the types of pamphlets or brochures you can ask for. (The United States government is the largest publisher in the country!)

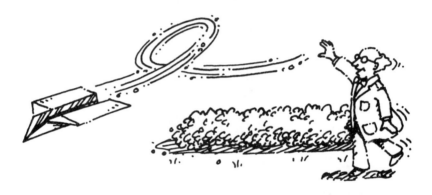

- **Businesses** are a good source of information. If you're interested in a particular type of business, don't be shy—write them for information. All big businesses (American Airlines, Porsche, Panasonic, Nintendo, Sony, Apple, etc.) have information they gladly send to interested people. You can find their addresses on the Internet, or ask your librarian for reference books that have business addresses.

- **Professional groups** (veterinarians, lawyers, police officers, airport managers, etc.) almost always have their own magazine. Professional magazines, called journals, contain articles and information of interest to people in those particular jobs.

- **Television** specials and documentaries are often loaded with interesting history and facts. If you see a show you like, you may be able to order a transcript (a written copy of what was said) by writing or calling the network.

- **Newsletters** from special interest groups and clubs have lots of up-to-date information. There are hundreds of such groups putting out newsletters including the *Ice Cream Reporters* and *Ghost Trackers Newsletter*. The Internet can guide you to many such groups. So can the publication *Newsletters in Print*, which you can find at any large library.

- **Public service organizations** are glad to send you information about their particular area. For example, these organizations (and many others) would be happy to send you material: American Cancer Society, American Horticultural Society, The Dinosaur Society, American Wildlife Federation, and League of Women Voters. Their addresses can be found in directories in the reference section of the library. Most large public service organizations also have Internet sites. Often you can send email to them via their Internet homepage.

Where to look for information: good bets and not-so-good bets

You might be thinking, "Yikes, too much stuff to look at! What kind of information do I really need?" That's a great question. One thing is for sure: You don't need to search everywhere for information about your topic.

For thousands of years, people had the problem of not enough information. These days we often have the problem of too much. Your job as a researcher is to figure out the best places to search for the information you need and to focus on those spots. Don't try to look everywhere, just look in places that will most likely lead to treasure.

What are those places? It depends on what type of research you're doing.

TOPIC:
  "The Early History of Our Town"
GOOD BET:
  the oldest available issues of your town newspaper
GOOD BET:
  your local historical society or museum
GOOD BET:
  books about your town or your state
BAD BET:
  an encyclopedia
  (Unless you live in a big city or a very famous city, your town is not likely to be listed in an encyclopedia.)

BAD BET:
> books about world history
> (World history is a huge topic. Finding information on
> your town would probably be like trying to find a needle
> in a haystack.)

TOPIC:
"The Celebration of Kwanza"
GOOD BET:
recently published books on African American culture
GOOD BET:
Ebony magazine
GOOD BET:
an Internet site on Kwanza or African American celebrations
BAD BET:
> books on Christmas celebrations and traditions
> (Kwanza starts the day after Christmas, but it doesn't
> have anything to do with Christmas.)
BAD BET:
> books on African culture 200 years ago
> (Kwanza is based on African traditions, but it was first
> celebrated in 1966.)

TOPIC:
"How Do Porpoises Communicate with One Another?"
GOOD BET:
an interview with someone who trains porpoises
GOOD BET:
a *National Geographic* video on porpoises
GOOD BET:
books and articles about porpoises and about animal
communications
BAD BET:
> an interview with the local zookeeper in charge of the
> eagles and falcons
> (The bird keeper may know very little about porpoises.)
BAD BET:
> magazines on sports fishing
> (People sport fish for mahi mahi, sometimes called

dolphins, but people do not fish for porpoises, which are also sometimes called dolphins.)

BAD BET:

books and articles about fish

(Porpoises are mammals, not fish.)

How will you know what's a good bet and what's a bad bet? Experience will be your guide after doing several research projects. Until then, don't hesitate to ask your teacher, parent, or librarian for advice.

BRAIN TICKLERS
Set #9

Before you go the library, think about what would be good places to find information. Where might you find information about these topics?

1. "The Weather and Atmosphere on Mars"
2. "The Top Three Money-Making Businesses in My Town"
3. "How Robots Are Being Used Today"
4. "The History of the Special Olympics"

(Answers on page 112.)

BRAIN TICKLERS—
THE ANSWERS

Set #8, page 104

1. Maria is unprepared for this interview. It is very hard for Ms. Lyon to give Maria clear answers when there are no clear questions. Maria should have taken time before the interview to think about exactly what information she wants to ask Ms. Lyon.

2. Tony asked the author, who is probably a busy woman, for her time, then insulted her by implying "I don't really care enough about this project to read your book." What if Tony had said, "I read your book and am very curious about the part where you discuss your climb on Mount Everest. Will you please tell me more about how the trekkers avoid frostbite and other physical dangers?" The author would surely have felt a lot better and would have been able to give Tony some wonderful information that would have made his research paper sparkle.

3. "How much do you like to eat sweets and do you let yourself eat too much?" is a confusing question—it uses words and ideas that kids could interpret in lots of different ways. Kids filling out Roxanne's questionnaire might have different definitions of "sweets" and of what quantity she means by "too much."

   Here is a much clearer way Roxanne might ask her question on a questionnaire:

   - How often do you eat sweets—candy, cookies, cake, doughnuts, pie, ice cream, frozen yogurt, sherbet, popsicles, or other snacks that contain sugar? Please choose one of the following answers:
         ____ less than once a week
         ____ less than once a day
         ____ once or twice a day
         ____ more than twice a day
         ____ I don't know.

- Do you think you eat too many sweets? Please choose one of the following answers:

  _____ I don't eat sweets at all.

  _____ I eat sweets but not too many.

  _____ I eat too many sweets.

  _____ I don't know.

Set #9, page 110

1. "The Weather and Atmosphere on Mars"

   Here are some good bets:

   - encyclopedias—look under "Mars," not "weather"
   - specialized encyclopedias about science or the universe
   - books about Mars
   - *Popular Science* and similar magazines
   - an interview with an astronomer if you know one
   - a trip to a nearby planetarium or science museum
   - the Internet: try http://www.atmos.washington.edu/mars.html

   Here are some not-so-good bets:

   - books about weather (These will almost certainly be about weather on earth.)
   - the weather channel on television (Not much there about Mars!)
   - books about the universe (Too broad; go for more specific sources first.)

2. "The Top Three Money-Making Businesses in My Town"

   Here are some good bets:

   - an interview with the mayor, a member of the town council, or someone at the local Chamber of Commerce
   - local newspaper articles
   - state or local business magazines
   - interviews with the owners or managers of these three businesses
   - publicity brochures from these three businesses

Here are some not-so-good bets:

- an interview with someone who recently got a job at one of these three businesses (That person probably doesn't know a lot about the business yet, although she might be able to tell you who does.)
- national business magazines (These are too broad unless one of the top three in your town is also one of the top businesses in the country.)
- books about successfully running your own small business (These would be how-to books, not books about specific successful businesses.)

3. "How Robots Are Being Used Today"

Here are some good bets:

- a TV special or documentary on robots
- newspaper or magazine articles on robots
- http://www.robotics.com/robots.html—that's an Internet site about robots

Here are some not-so-good bets:

- science fiction books (They may talk about robots, but not about how they are actually used today.)
- books about 19th-century inventors and inventions (Robots are 20th-century creations.)
- science books published five or ten years ago (This is such a rapidly developing field that you need very current information.)

4. "The History of the Special Olympics"

Here are some good bets:

- brochures published by the Special Olympics
- information from the Special Olympics site on the Internet at http://www.specialolympics.org
- magazine articles about athletic programs for handicapped kids
- an interview with someone who works in the public relations office of the Special Olympics

Here are some not-so-good bets:

- magazine articles on sports in colonial America (The Special Olympics didn't exist back then.)
- books and articles on professional sports and professional athletes (The Special Olympics is designed for amateurs, not pros.)
- books on physical education for middle school students (The Special Olympics is for handicapped athletes of all ages, not just middle school. Also, it is not operated by the school system.)

CHAPTER FIVE

Taking Notes

You've found the treasure! It took a little digging, but now you have books, articles, and other sources of information about your topic. This chapter is about what to do with those sources: picking the best ones, writing down information about those sources, and taking notes on all the interesting things you learn.

USING NOTE CARDS

Unless you have a photographic memory, you won't be able to remember everything you read, even if you are doing research for a short paper. You need to take notes. The best way is to write down the facts you learn on 3×5 or 4×6 note cards (3-by-5's are 3 inches long and 5 inches wide; 4-by-6's are 4 inches long and 6 inches wide).

Why are note cards better than notebook paper for keeping notes? If you write all your notes on a few sheets of notebook paper, it's very hard to organize your information later. If you write each piece of information on separate note cards, however, you can organize by sorting the cards, and you can keep resorting and reorganizing until you like the order. (We'll see how that's done in Chapter Six.) You can also sort and organize if you take notes on a computer word processing program, but it might be more confusing for your first few projects. Start with note cards—they'll make your job much simpler.

DETERMINING IF A SOURCE WILL BE HELPFUL

Before you start taking notes, ask whether the book (or newspaper article or any other source) is even worth taking notes on. Often students are so afraid they won't be able to find information on their topic that they frantically start taking notes from whatever book they find first. Don't fall into that trap—it can be a waste of time.

Pull a book off the library shelf and look at the first few pages (the table of contents) and the last few pages (the index). Ask yourself an important question: Does this book talk about *exactly* what I want to know?

Imagine that you recently learned that a plant called Venus's-flytrap catches insects and eats them. That sounds kind of weird, so you want to know more. You find a book in the library called *Meat-Eating Plants* by Nathan Aaseng. You look at the table of contents to see whether this book will be useful. How does this look to you?

CONTENTS
1. Green Monsters and Killer Fungi ... 5
2. Flypaper Traps ... 13
3. Pitfall Traps ... 21
4. Trigger Traps ... 29
5. Endless Quest for Survival ... 35
Notes by Chapter ... 43
Glossary ... 44
Classification ... 45
Further Reading ... 46
Index ... 47

Do you think Chapter 2 is about Venus's-flytraps? It looks like it is, but you can't be sure unless you flip to the index. This is what you see in the index under "V":

V
Venus's-flytrap (*Dionaea*), 4, 7, 28–31, 38, 42
    flower, 30
    location, 29
    trapping, 30–31

Yes, this book does have information about Venus's-flytrap, so it is probably a very good source for your research. But wait a minute—the information about Venus's-flytrap is not in Chapter 2 (pages 13–20) after all. It's mostly in the chapter about trigger traps (pages 29–34). Get used to using the indexes of books—they are very useful in deciding whether a particular book will be helpful in your research and knowing which pages of the book you need to read.

Here are two more tips for determining whether a source will be useful for your research:

- **Is this source up to date?** Between 1912 and 1959 there were only 48 states in the United States. Until Hawaii and Alaska became states, all books and articles said that we had 48 states, and they were correct. Now that "fact" is very wrong. Until 1991 Russia was a part of the Soviet Union. Now there is no Soviet Union. If you are studying about the modern Russian government, books or articles written before 1991 would be of limited use.

- **Is the source fair?** Does it talk about all sides of an issue or does it give only one side of the issue? Is it discriminatory against anybody or any idea? Some books and magazines are very biased toward one idea or another. Perhaps one is very anti-Republican and another very anti-Democrat. A magazine article might be very pro-environment while another is very pro-development. When you read, try to determine whether you're getting the whole story or just one side of the story.

Making source cards

When you find a book, article, encyclopedia, or any other source that has some interesting information, the first thing to do is take out a note card and write down some information about that source. We'll call these "source cards." Your source cards are very important—they are your reminder of what books you've looked through, what articles you've read, and where you got your information. Think of them as torches lighting your way into a cave of knowledge.

Make a source card for every book, Internet site, brochure, or any other type of material you read for your research, even if you don't take any notes from that source. Why? First, some teachers want to know about everything you read, whether or not you take any notes or use any of the information in your project. Second, knowing what you've already read keeps you from going back to unhelpful sources. Third, your source cards tell you what information to put in your bibliography—a list at the end of your paper that shows your reader all the sources you used in your research. To see what a bibliography looks like, turn to page 217.

Where do you find the information to put on these source cards? If you use an index such as *Reader's Guide* or a database such as SIRS, all the information you need is right there with each entry. If you use a book or encyclopedia, the information you need is on the title page at the front of the book or on the copyright page, which follows the title page.

This is what a source card would look like for a book:

Source card for a book with one author

Author	Gonick, Larry
Title of book	The Cartoon History of the Universe
City where published	New York
Name of publisher	Doubleday
Year published	1994

This is what a source card would look like for a magazine article:

Source card for a magazine article

Author	Hound, Basset
Title of article	"Playing Ping-Pong with your dog"
Magazine	Dog Days Magazine
Month and year	November 1996
Page numbers	1-5

In Appendix B on page 225, we have included forms that you can use to gather information from many kinds of reference sources. There are blank source cards for newspaper articles, videos, CD-ROMs, encyclopedias, and more. You can photocopy these blank forms and use them as you gather information for your research project and as you write your bibliography.

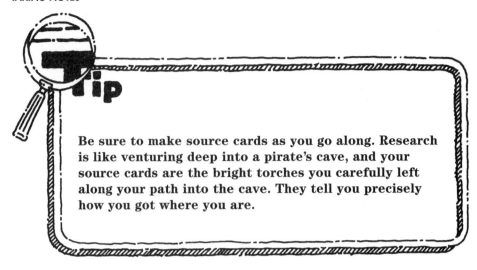

Be sure to make source cards as you go along. Research is like venturing deep into a pirate's cave, and your source cards are the bright torches you carefully left along your path into the cave. They tell you precisely how you got where you are.

THINK—DON'T COPY!

Call the cops! Copying is a cop-out. It's illegal, too.

When you were younger, you might have thought that research meant copying information from an encyclopedia. That's not research at all. Copying someone else's work and presenting it as your own is called plagiarism, and it's against the law.

If you copy a bunch of information from *The World Book Encyclopedia* and turn it in, you haven't done a research project. You've shown your teacher that you can copy, but you haven't shown her that you can think and organize ideas. Research is not about copying. It's about searching for information that answers your questions, then organizing and expressing that information in a way that is truly your own. Resist the temptation to copy information from books or other sources. Read the information, think, then put what you have read into your own words.

When you write notes in your own words from the information you read, you're doing more than avoiding the plagiarism police. In fact, you're doing the very essence of research: you're finding facts and expressing them in your own way. Take the time while you're taking notes to express ideas in your own words. Later when you write your paper, you'll thank yourself a thousand times because writing will be a thousand times easier.

Sometimes you will want to quote someone else. In that case, it's fine to copy exactly what someone else wrote, but be sure to use quotation marks when you take notes and when you write your paper. Those quotation marks say, "I'm repeating *exactly* what someone else said or wrote."

Caution! Major mistake territory!

Don't be guilty of plagiarism! If you have reason to copy, always use quotation marks on your note cards. When you begin writing your paper, it's very easy to forget that those were someone else's words if there are no quotation marks on the note card.

Printing, scanning, downloading, and photocopying

There are times when you want to photocopy a magazine article at the library and bring it home to read later. Or you might want to download an article from the Internet and read it later. You might print out something from an encyclopedia on CD-ROM or scan a newspaper article into your computer. All these techniques can save you a lot of time. But if you're not careful, they become just fancy forms of copying. Instead of being a high-tech researcher, you're guilty of kindergarten research (copy, copy, copy). Even worse, you might be guilty of plagiarism.

If you do photocopy, download, print, or scan, you still need to take notes—*in your own words!* Carefully read the material, think about what you've read, and write some clear and simple phrases to describe it. This way, the research becomes your work, not someone else's.

How to take good notes

Let's say you're doing a research report on koala bears. You go to the library and discover where *The World Book Encyclopedia* is kept. You pull down the "K" volume and on page 360 you find this:

> Koala, *koh AH luh*, is an Australian mammal that looks like a teddy bear. It is sometimes called a koala bear or native bear, but the koala is not related to any kind of bear. Koalas have soft, thick fur; a large, hairless nose; round ears; and no tail. The fur is gray or brown on the animal's back and white on the belly. Koalas measure from 25 to 30 inches in length and weigh 15 to 30 pounds. Koalas have sharp, curved claws; long toes; and a strong grip. They spend nearly all their time in trees and come down only to move to another one. Koalas are active mainly at night. They sleep most of the day in the fork of a eucalyptus tree. Koalas eat mainly the leaves and young shoots of eucalyptus trees. They obtain liquids chiefly from eucalyptus leaves. Koalas that live in the

wild rarely drink water. The word *koala* comes from an Australian Aborigine word meaning *no drink.*

Koalas are marsupials. Female koalas give birth to tiny, poorly developed offspring. The young koala, called a *joey,* is carried in a pouch on its mother's belly until it develops more completely. It remains in the pouch for about seven months, suckling on one of the mother's two nipples. It spends the next six months riding on its mother's back.

At one time, koalas were hunted for their fur. By the 1920s, the animals had been almost wiped out by hunters. Since then, killing of koalas has been prohibited by law. But the koala population has continued to decline. People have cut down eucalyptus forests for housing developments, resorts, and farmland. Many koalas are hit by cars. In addition, much of the koala population is infected by *chlamydia,* a disease that can cause blindness, infertility in females, and pneumonia. Australian and international conservation organizations are working to counteract the effects of the disease.

That's what the 1996 edition of *The World Book Encyclopedia* says about koalas. Now, how do you collect the information that you need? Here's an example of how you could write note cards on this information.

<u>How do they look?</u>　　　World Book, 360
like a teddy bear
soft, thick fur—gray or brown on their backs
    and white on their bellies
no tail
no hair on their noses
round ears

How big are they?   World Book, 360
25–30 inches long
15–30 pounds

What are they?   World Book, 360
mammals, but not kin to any kind of bear
marsupials—mother carries the joey in a
     pouch for about 7 months
babies ride on moms' backs for about 6 more
     months

Where do they live?   World Book, 360
live in Australia
they live in trees

<u>How do they live?</u>   World Book, 360
they sleep almost all day and move around at
   night

<u>What's their diet?</u>   World Book, 360
eat leaves of trees, especially eucalyptus
name "koala" means "no drink" because they
   rarely drink water; they get their water
   from the leaves they eat

<u>Are they okay?</u>   World Book, 360
people used to hunt them for fur
hunting is illegal; now get hit by cars
also get diseases—scientists are trying to
   find solutions

Guidelines for good note-taking

- **Write the main idea.** The underlined words in the top left corner of each of these note cards about koalas is the main idea or the question being answered. It tells you what that card is about. Writing the main idea in the corner helps in two ways. First, it keeps you on track while you take notes, reminding you *exactly* what information you're after. Second, it helps you sort and organize your note cards when it's time to write. (We'll talk more about that in Chapter Six.)

- **Include only one main idea per card.** All the notes on a particular card give information about one main idea or answer one question. If you put lots of different ideas on the same card, your note cards will be harder to organize later.

- **Use your own words.** Notice that all these notes on koalas are in our own words. We haven't copied any sentences word for word from the encyclopedia.

- **Keep it short.** Write your notes in short, simple phrases. This saves time and helps avoid copying. You can construct longer, fancier sentences later when it's time to write the paper.

- **Include the source and page number.** *World Book* in the top right means that the information on these cards came from *The World Book Encyclopedia*, and *360* means that these notes came from page 360 of that source. If you make a mistake on a note card and need to go back to the library to look up that information again, you'll know exactly where to look. More importantly, your teacher may require you to include footnotes or endnotes in your paper, showing exactly where particular facts came from.

Tip

Pick a key word or two from the title of the source that lets you identify it on note cards. If you are using more than one encyclopedia, be sure not to use just the word *encyclopedia* on your note cards. That's a sure way to get your sources mixed up.

Guidelines for good note-taking (continued)

- **Write only as much as you need.** Sometimes the key to being a good researcher is to work less. (Yes, you read those words correctly: *work less.*) One mistake students often make is to write lots of information that has nothing to do with their topic. If your project is about mammals in the United States that are nearly extinct, there's no reason to collect information about any of these:

  - nearly extinct birds (they aren't mammals)
  - nearly extinct snakes (they aren't mammals either)
  - nearly extinct mammals in South America
  - animals that used to be nearly extinct but aren't anymore
  - animals that are extinct

  Using your search plan as your guide, think about what questions you really need to answer. Then answer just those questions, not every question in the world! Take aim, zero in on exactly what you need, and you'll hit a bull's eye every time.

BRAIN TICKLERS
Set #10

1. Remember your research about plants that eat bugs? Here are the tables of contents of two more books you found in the library. Do they look useful for this research?

The first book is *Carnivorous Plants* by Nancy J. Nielsen.

The second book is *More Plants That Changed History* by Joan Elma Rahn.

2. You're writing a report called "The History of In-Line Skating." You tell the library computer to search for books on "skating" and find this book. Do you think it would be helpful in your research?

> Title: *Roller Skating in America*
> Author: Smith, William
> Summary: Discusses the history of roller
>   skating in the U.S.
>
> Smith, William
>   *Roller Skating in America.*—Smith, William.—
>   New York: Sports Press, 1950.
>
> Discusses the history of roller skating in
> the U.S.
>
> 1. Skating   2. Roller skating   3. Sports

3. Monica's teacher wants the class to tackle an issue that is highly controversial (something people have very strong feelings and strong disagreements about). The assignment is to compare opinions for and against the issue, being as fair as possible, not taking sides one way or the other. Monica decides to write about whether the driving age should be raised to 18. She finds three articles published in *Seventeen* magazine then writes her report based on these three articles. Can you see a problem with her approach?

4. Here's what the book *Why Things Are* says about toe shoes for ballerinas:

> Toe shoes, with square solid toes, are used by ballerinas who dance on the tips of their toes, a position known as *on pointe*. The peculiar shape of these shoes makes it easier for them to balance.

Here's what Susie wrote in her paper:

> Toe shoes have square solid toes and are used by ballerinas who dance on the tips of their toes. This position is known as *on pointe*. The peculiar shape of toe shoes makes it easier for ballerinas to balance.

What mistake did Susie make?

5. Lance's topic is America's favorite sports in the early 20th century. His library has a copy of the book *The Fastest Bicycle Rider in the World*, which is an autobiography by Marshall W. Taylor. (An autobiography is a book the author has written about himself or herself.) Taylor was a world-famous bicycle racer who began competing in the 1890s. He was also the first African American to become a sports champion in this country. Lance looks in the introduction on page vii and reads this:

> Remember bike racing? Bike racing on the old board tracks: Probably not. Not many do these days. But there was an age when it rivaled baseball and boxing in popularity. It was a spectacle—fast, dangerous, and colorful.

> In its heyday of the Roaring Twenties, the six-day races played to packed houses and produced million dollar weeks for the great city arenas like Madison Square Garden. Throughout the East, the South, the Midwest, and the Pacific Coast there were professional racing

circuits. Any city worth the name had a bicycle track, and the fans eagerly squeezed themselves into its wooden grandstand to watch the races.

Here are the notes Lance took on these two paragraphs. What problems do you see with each note card and how would you improve each one?

CARD 1:

> **What sports start**
> **with the letter "B"?**   Fastest, vii
>
> baseball, boxing, bicycle racing

CARD 2:

> **What was bike racing like?**
>
> It was a spectacle—fast, dangerous, and colorful.

CARD 3:

> How popular was bike racing?   Fastest, vii
>
> as popular as baseball and boxing
> raced on old board tracks
> big tracks earned a million dollars a week
> tracks in every big city in the country
> races would last for 6 days
> very popular in the 1920s

6. Here's a copyright page from a book you're using for your project. Can you find all the information you need to fill out a source card?

Copyright © 1997 by Rebecca Elliott
Illustrations copyright © 1997 by Laurie Hamilton

All rights reserved. No part of this book may be reproduced in any form, by photostat, microfilm, xerography, or any other means, or incorporated into any information retrieval system, electronic or mechanical, without the written permission of the copyright owner.

All inquiries should be addressed to:
Barron's Educational Series, Inc.
250 Wireless Boulevard
Hauppauge, New York 11788

International Standard Book No. 0-8120-9781-5

Library of Congress Catalog Card No. 97-7370

Library of Congress Cataloging-in-Publication Data

Elliott, Rebecca, 1948–
    Painless grammar / by Rebecca Elliott ; illustrated by
    Laurie Hamilton

Includes index.
ISBN 0-8120-9781-5
1. English language—Grammar—Study and teaching I. Title
LB1576.E45 1997
428'.007—dc21   97-7370
                                                      CIP

PRINTED IN THE UNITED STATES OF AMERICA
9 8 7 6 5 4 3 2 1

BRAIN TICKLERS— THE ANSWERS

Set #10, page 130

1. In the first book, Chapter 2 looks perfect since you're interested specifically in Venus's-flytraps. The second book looks interesting, but it's not right on track. It might be great for a future project, but not for this one.

   Don't spend a lot of time with books and other sources that aren't quite on track. Keep looking until you find information that is exactly what you need.

2. This book is probably not useful. Check the date it was published. In-line skates didn't exist in 1950.

   Don't give up if you don't find gold the first time you dig. Keep looking. Treasure is there—you just might have to dig a little to find it.

3. There's absolutely nothing wrong with Monica's reading those three articles in *Seventeen*, but this paper is supposed to be about pros and cons. That means she needs to read about and include in her paper all sides of the argument. *Seventeen* is written mainly for teenagers, so its articles might have a very teen-oriented perspective. Monica should look up information about the subject in a few other magazines and newspapers as well so she'll have a more complete view of the issue.

4. Call the cops! Susie is guilty of plagiarism. She changed a word or two in this paragraph, but not much. There are many ways she could put this information in her own words. Here's one way:

> Ballerinas wear shoes called toe shoes. These shoes look a little odd. They are shaped oddly with square solid toes because of the job they do: they help the dancer balance on the tips of her toes. This position on the tips of the toes is called *on pointe*.

5. Card 1: Lance's topic is America's favorite sports in the early 20th century. Does it really matter that some sports of that era begin with the letter "b"? Lance can avoid wasting time if he doesn't take notes on information that has nothing to do with his main idea.

Card 2: There are two big problems here. First, there's no way to tell where this information came from because there's nothing in the right hand corner. If the teacher requires footnotes or endnotes, Lance can't use this information at all because he can't document where it came from. Second, this is either kindergarten copying or it's a direct quote from the author. If it's a quote, it should have quotation marks around it. Lance probably won't remember that these are not his words when he writes his paper.

Either of these note cards is fine:

<u>What was bike racing like?</u>　　　　Fastest, vii

"It was a spectacle—fast, dangerous, and colorful."

What was bike racing like?   Fastest, vii

fast, dangerous, exciting
lots of crowd appeal
festive atmosphere

Card 3: This card is supposed to be about "how popular was bike racing?" but it has information about other key ideas as well. Organizing these note cards (that will be the next step in the research process) would be much easier if the information were written on two or more cards, perhaps like this:

How popular was bike racing?   Fastest, vii

as popular as baseball and boxing
big tracks earned a million dollars a week
tracks in every big city in the country
very popular in the 1920s

What were races like?   Fastest, vii

raced on old board tracks
races would last for 6 days

6. This is how your source card for this book would look:

Source card for a book or pamphlet with one author	
Author	Elliott, Rebecca
Title of book	Painless Grammar
City where published	Hauppauge, NY
Name of publisher	Barron's Educational Series, Inc.
Year published	1997

CHAPTER SIX

What to Do with Your Treasure

Now that you have collected your treasure, what are you going to do with it? Show it off, of course. With a research project, showing off your treasure might mean using the information you found to write a short play. It might mean drawing maps or diagrams about what you learned. Maybe it means creating a series of posters or doing a science demonstration. No matter how you show off your treasure, your teacher will usually want you to include a written report. This chapter and the next two are about how to turn your note cards into a clear, interesting, well-organized paper.

ORGANIZING YOUR KEY IDEAS

Sit down at a large table or on the floor where you have plenty of room to spread out. Your mission is to take all your note cards and divide them into several piles. Each pile will be made up of cards about a key idea.

Let's imagine you've been working on that project about your math teacher's part-time job as a lion trainer. Remember the key ideas we came up with earlier?

KEY IDEA A: ABOUT MY MATH TEACHER
Where did my math teacher grow up?
How did she get interested in lion training?
Where does my math teacher work as a lion trainer?
What do my math teacher's family and friends think about her part-time job?

KEY IDEA B: ABOUT LION TRAINING AND LION TRAINERS
How many trained lions are there in this country?
Who is the most famous lion trainer of all time?
How long does it take to become a lion trainer?

KEY IDEA C: DANGERS OF THE JOB
Has my teacher ever gotten hurt by a lion?
How often do lion trainers get hurt?

KEY IDEA D: WHAT'S THE LION TRAINER'S MAGIC TOUCH?
What are their secrets with the lions?

KEY IDEA E: MY MATH TEACHER'S TWO DIFFERENT JOBS
Does she like both her jobs?
Does she like lion training more than teaching math? How are her two jobs different?

You interviewed your math teacher and read two magazine articles about lion training. You found a book in the library on circus animals and took some notes from that. You even found a site on the Internet that had information on training circus animals.

You found some very interesting facts, and you wrote your information on 20 or 30 note cards. Now they are all spread out in front of you. Put all the note cards with information "about my math teacher" into pile number 1. Put all the cards with information "about lion training and lion trainers" into pile number 2. Put all the cards with information about "dangers of the job" into pile number 3, and so on. If you aren't sure yet where a card belongs, put it into a wait-and-see pile.

<u>what does her family think?</u>   interview

Her mom has mixed feelings—thinks it's great
and is very proud—but scared Ms. L will get
hurt by a lion.

Her dad is jealous—thinks it's a super exciting
job—wants her to teach him to do lion training

If you wrote titles for your note cards (like "what does her family think?" in the left corner of this card), sorting the cards into piles will be easy. This card obviously goes into the Key Idea A pile. If you didn't write titles, read each card carefully and decide where it best fits.

Make a new note card to use as a label for each pile. The label card for pile number 1 would be "about my math teacher." The label card for pile number 2 would be "about lion training and lion trainers," and so on. Put the label card on top of the pile, then put a rubber band around each pile to keep the cards from coming loose.

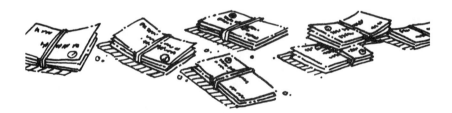

Let's imagine that as you did your research, three interesting new questions came up and you took notes about them. Here are the three new questions that you found answers for:

1. How and where do lion trainers learn their skill?
2. Does a lion trainer always work with the same lions or could he or she work with any cage full of lions?
3. What is the hardest part about training and handling the lions?

Where does this new information best fit? Question 1 would probably fit best in the pile "about lion training and lion trainers." Question 2 would also fit well in that pile. Question 3 could fit with either "about lion training and lion trainers" or "what's the lion trainer's magic touch?" Let's put it in the "magic touch" pile.

Tips for organizing your key ideas

Next, line up the piles of note cards; any order is okay at first. Read your label cards from left to right. If you were to write the paper in that order, does it sound good to you? Does the order makes sense? No? Then rearrange the piles and read your label cards again. Keep doing this until you like the order and it tells the story well.

There is only one rule when it comes to putting your piles in order: If that order doesn't make sense or will confuse your reader, try a different order.

Are these ideas in a good order?

1. Dangers of the job
2. About lion training and lion trainers
3. What is the lion trainer's magic touch?
4. My teacher's two different jobs
5. About my math teacher

This paper is about Ms. Lyon—she's the main character—so it probably doesn't make sense to introduce her to the reader at the very end of the paper.

Is this a good order?

1. About my math teacher
2. Dangers of the job
3. My teacher's two different jobs
4. About lion training and lion trainers
5. What is the lion trainer's magic touch?

It doesn't make sense to talk about the dangers of the job before talking about the job itself.

Keep moving the stacks around until you have an order that you think tells the story in a clear and interesting way. Arrange and rearrange. Don't stop until you like the order. All that rearranging is doing more than moving around the dust on top of your desk. It's making you think! Once you've put your cards in order, you know very clearly how your story is going to unfold, and writing your report will be much easier.

For this paper, this would be a good order:

1. About my math teacher
2. My teacher's two different jobs
3. About lion training and lion trainers
4. Dangers of the job
5. What is the lion trainer's magic touch?

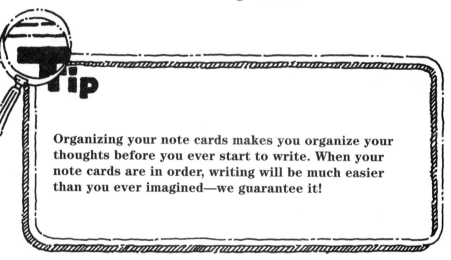

Tip

Organizing your note cards makes you organize your thoughts before you ever start to write. When your note cards are in order, writing will be much easier than you ever imagined—we guarantee it!

If you have trouble putting your key idea stacks in order, pretend you're telling a friend the story of what you discovered on your treasure hunt. It's just like telling an exciting mystery story, a romance, or a ghost story. How would you tell a really juicy story to your best friend?

A good story can unfold in many different ways. Here are some examples:

- **Chronological order:** Some stories unfold best when they go in chronological order: first this happened, then that happened, then the next thing happened. If you're writing about a famous person's life or a particular event in history, this order often works well.

- **Question-Answer:** Some stories work well in a question and answer format. This might be good if you are writing, for example, about the best ways to train a puppy. What works best for paper training? What works best for teaching the puppy to stay? What works best for house breaking as the puppy gets older?

- **Similarities-Differences:** Some stories work well when you first present the similarities between two things, people, or ideas, then the differences—or the other way around. This is a good order if you are writing about two candidates running for president or a comparison between soccer and football.

- **For-Against:** Some stories work well when you present all the reasons for a particular issue, then all the reasons against it. If you are writing about extending the school year, providing free french fries with school lunch, or some other hot issue, this might be a good order.

- **Problems-Solutions:** Some stories work well when you talk about a problem, then you talk about various solutions. If you're writing about illegal drugs or air pollution, this type of order might be good.

Sorting your note cards

Now that you have your key idea stacks in order, it's time to organize the cards in each stack. Take the rubber band off the first stack and spread out all the cards in that stack.

If you took notes on your computer instead of on note cards, print out all your notes. Then use scissors to separate one idea from another. You are making your own note cards. They won't all be the same size, but you can still sort them and organize them. This will be much easier than trying to organize them on the computer using cut and paste functions.

Imagine that you're organizing the cards in the first stack for the paper about Ms. Lyon. (The first stack is labeled "about my math teacher.") You might have two or three cards with information about what Ms. Lyon's family thinks about her job, one or two cards with information about how she got interested in lion training, and so on. Your job is to put these cards in order in a way that is clear and interesting.

Is this order clear?

1. What do my math teacher's family and friends think about her part-time job?
2. How did she get interested in lion training?
3. Where does my math teacher work as a lion trainer?
4. Where did my math teacher grow up?

That order is confusing because it talks about what Ms. Lyon's family and friends think of her job before talking about what that job is. Shuffle the cards around until you have an order that tells that part of the story well. Several different orders could work. Here's one:

1. Where did my math teacher grow up?
2. How did she get interested in lion training?
3. Where does my math teacher work as a lion trainer?
4. What do my math teacher's family and friends think about her part-time job?

This order tells Ms. Lyon's story chronologically.

When all the cards in one stack are organized in a way that you like, put the label card back on the front of the stack, put the rubber band around it, and put it aside. Take out the next stack and organize the cards in it.

What to do with your extra note cards

There's just one more step in sorting your cards, and it's an easy one. Pull out the stack of extra cards that you couldn't decide where to put. Do some of them fit well into the piles you have made? If so, put them into those piles. Place them in the order they fit best.

Can some of them join together to make a new key idea? If so, put them together into a new pile and put a label card on top. Where would that new pile best fit into the order? Put it there.

Don't worry about the cards that don't seem to fit anywhere. Gather them in a pile labeled "probably not needed" or "wait and see." As you write you'll find spots to slip in an interesting example, story, or fact from your "wait-and-see" pile. Some cards won't find a home in your paper, but never feel bad about taking a few more notes than you need. Good researchers always gather more interesting information than they can use in their papers. It's like having some money in savings—it's there if you need it.

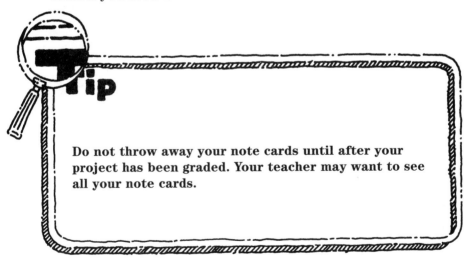

Tip

Do not throw away your note cards until after your project has been graded. Your teacher may want to see all your note cards.

A painless outline

Getting all your note cards in order makes you do a lot of thinking about the best way to write your paper or present your project. In fact, as you organize your cards, you are actually making an outline.

Some teachers want to see an outline. All you have to do is go through your organized note cards, write down your key ideas, and list the main questions or topics under each key idea. Here is how that would look for the project about Ms. Lyon:

I. About my math teacher
   A. Where did my math teacher grow up?
   B. How did she get interested in lion training?
   C. Where does my math teacher work as a lion trainer?
   D. What do my math teacher's family and friends think about her part-time job?
II. My math teacher's two different jobs
   A. Does she like both her jobs?
   B. Does she like lion training more than teaching math? How are her two jobs different?
III. About lion training and lion trainers
   A. How and where do lion trainers learn their skill?
   B. How long does it take to become a lion trainer?
   C. Who is the most famous lion trainer of all time?
   D. How many trained lions are there in this country?
   E. Does a lion trainer always work with the same lions or could he or she work with any cage full of lions?
IV. Dangers of the job
   A. How often do lion trainers get hurt?
   B. Has my teacher ever gotten hurt by a lion?
V. What's the lion trainer's magic touch?
   A. What is the hardest part about training and handling the lions?
   B. What are their secrets with the lions?

By doing such good organizing ahead of time, your paper is more than halfway finished. The next step will be to get those well-organized thoughts down on paper.

BRAIN TICKLERS
Set #11

1. Justin's paper is titled "The 1871 Fire That Almost Destroyed Chicago." Justin put all his note cards in piles of five key ideas, then he put the five piles in this order. Do you think this is a good order? How would you suggest that Justin change the order?

   1. Rebuilding the city of Chicago
   2. The extent of the destruction
   3. How long the fire raged
   4. How a cow kicked over a lantern in a barn to start the fire
   5. Chicago before the fire

2. Julie is writing a report on how the biggest diamonds in the world were mined. She found some great information in the library. She saw an exhibit at the Smithsonian Institution in Washington and bought some fabulous picture postcards of huge diamonds. When she came home, she interviewed her neighbor who is a jeweler and who knows a lot about diamonds and other precious stones. Julie took lots of very interesting notes on 3×5 note cards. She sat down at her dad's computer with a pile of 40 note cards and started writing her paper. Before long she felt very frustrated. Can you see what Julie could have done to make writing much easier and more pleasant for herself?

(Answers on page 181.)

Writing your rough draft

Your note cards are well organized, and now it's time to write. The first version of your report is called the rough draft. That's because it should be rough, not smooth and polished.

Polishing comes later. The first version can be sloppy and full of spelling "errrorrs." It can have the words *a lot* spelled "alot" and it can even have dumb sentences like this: "It's rough to write a rough draft about roughing it in the woods on a cold night sleeping under a rough wool blanket with your dog going ruff-ruff all night."

If you've ever baked a cake, built a model airplane, planted a garden, or painted a picture, you know that when you do a creative project, you often make a mess in the short run. That's part of the process—even part of the fun. Creativity and messes go hand in hand. Clean-up can be very creative, too, but that comes later.

Caution! Major mistake territory!

Don't even think of trying to make your first draft perfect. Trying to get it just right on your first try is a sure way to make yourself feel like a failure. No professional writer expects a first effort to be perfect. If you want to be a good writer, you gotta rough it.

THE INTRODUCTION: WHERE IT ALL STARTS

The introduction is the first few sentences or paragraphs of your paper. It tells your reader what to expect and what this paper is going to be about. A boring introduction gets the paper off to a boring and often confusing start. A clear, concise, clever introduction is like the opening scenes of a really good movie; it grabs attention and makes your reader want to know more.

The key to writing a good introduction is this: Be very clear what your main idea is. Clear away all the fog in your brain. When your main idea is crystal clear in your mind, think up the most interesting, funniest, scariest, or most creative sentence you can about that main idea. Write it down. Think up another and write that sentence, too. Write every interesting introduction you can think of. Later you can pick the one you like the best for the introduction. Some of the sentences you don't use for the introduction may find a home elsewhere in your paper.

Let's imagine your project is about porpoises. What is your main idea? What precisely are you writing about? Here are some possible main ideas:

- Porpoises are very intelligent animals—far more intelligent than most people believe.
- Porpoises are endangered by many fishing practices, and they need our help.
- Porpoises have some of the most interesting communication skills of any creatures in the sea.

Can you see that even though each of these papers is about porpoises, the main idea is quite different in each one? Notice in the following examples that if you don't have a sharp focus on the main idea, the introduction is about as exciting as a bowl of yesterday morning's soggy cereal.

UNFOCUSED INTRODUCTION:

Porpoises live in the sea and are smarter than tunas.
(The reader does not have a clear idea what this paper is going to be about.)

FOCUSED INTRODUCTION:

Of all the creatures that live in the ocean, porpoises are perhaps the most intelligent. You might even call them the brainiacs of the sea.
(Now the reader has a very clear idea what you'll be talking about.)

UNFOCUSED INTRODUCTION:

Porpoises are sometimes called dolphins, but people don't eat them.

FOCUSED INTRODUCTION:

Porpoises are not fished for food, yet they often end up tangled and mangled in the nets of fishermen.
Fortunately, recent laws are helping protect them from this sad fate.

UNFOCUSED INTRODUCTION:

This paper is about porpoise noises.

FOCUSED INTRODUCTION:

I have always liked to stand on the beach watching porpoises frolic in the waves, but I never knew that these graceful, playful animals "talk" to each other. This paper is about what I learned by interviewing an ocean scientist.

The introduction doesn't have to be long. If your paper is short (three pages or so), your introduction should probably be only one paragraph. If your paper is eight or ten pages long, you might want to write a longer introduction, but it shouldn't take more than two or three paragraphs to get your teacher and other readers interested in your topic and let them know what you are writing about.

Writing successful introductions

Your paper could have many different types of introductions, any one of which would be fine. The introduction could be serious or light-hearted, depending on the feeling you want to give in your paper. Here are some ways you might write an interesting introduction:

Ask a question

DULL:

Does our city's river have pollution in it?

INTERESTING:

If your throat were parched with thirst, would you dip your cup into our city's river for a refreshing drink?

Draw an interesting picture with your words

DULL:

Cheetahs run fast.

INTERESTING:

Imagine a big cat racing down the highway at 60 miles per hour keeping up with Fords and Ferraris. Impossible? Not if that cat is a cheetah.

Tell a very short story that introduces what your report is about

DULL:

Many kids in our school participate in volunteer activities after school.

INTERESTING:

Every Tuesday after school, Martina Sanchez goes to the hospital. She isn't sick. In fact, she goes to the hospital to help prevent sickness. She helps teach young children in an afterschool program about disease prevention and good health.

Tell your reader a very interesting fact, maybe even a shocking one

DULL:

Acid rain causes a lot of problems.

INTERESTING:

Acid rain has been blamed by some scientists for the extinction of the dinosaurs. Although that theory is hotly debated, there is no question that acid rain is a great threat to our forests today. If our forests are not to end up like the dinosaurs, we need to understand more about what causes acid rain, how to prevent it, and how to repair the damage it has done.

Make a strong statement of your main idea

DULL:

Cigarettes are unhealthy and people who smoke should quit.

INTERESTING:

Until the mid-1980s, the most common fatal cancer was stomach cancer. Cigarettes changed that. As smoking increased, so did lung cancer. Now lung cancer is the most common fatal cancer. Smoking is a killer—a totally preventable one.

THE BODY: TURNING NOTE CARDS INTO PARAGRAPHS

Uh-oh. Paragraphs—those monsters of writing. Wait a minute! You don't need to be afraid of paragraphs because you are well prepared. Remember all that work you did organizing your note cards? You were doing more than shuffling paper— you were actually organizing your thoughts into paragraphs.

A good paragraph can be as simple as one main idea with smaller ideas following it. Think of a mother elephant with a bunch of baby elephants following behind her. The first sentence of the paragraph (the mother elephant) gives a fact, an idea, or an opinion. The other sentences (the little elephants) give reasons, examples, extra facts, or maybe short stories about the main idea.

Let's see how to turn note cards into paragraphs. Do you remember the Hale-Bopp comet that was so bright in the sky in 1997? Did you go outside on clear nights to examine its long tail through binoculars? Imagine that you got very curious about comets, and now you are doing a project about them. When you organized your ideas and questions, you came up with these key ideas:

KEY IDEA A:
  What is a comet made of?
KEY IDEA B:
  How big are comets?
KEY IDEA C:
  How do comets travel? Where do they go?

You have done your research and organized your note cards. It's time to write. You take the rubber band off the pile labeled "Key Idea A." Here are the note cards you wrote about Key Idea A (What is a comet made of?) while you were doing the research. (Notice that none of these note cards about comets has a page number. That's because all this information came from CD-ROMs, which don't have page numbers. One is *The New Grolier Multimedia Encyclopedia*, the other is called *Microsoft Bookshelf* and is a combination encyclopedia, atlas, almanac, and dictionary.)

<u>What are comets made of?</u>   MS-Bookshelf

some people call them dirty snowballs because they are made of water, carbon dioxide, ammonia, and methane, all frozen and mixed with grit and dust

<u>What makes tails?</u>   MS-Bookshelf

tail made up of gas and dust particles

<u>Why *do* tails point?</u>   MS-Bookshelf

tail always points away from the sun because
the gases and particles are pushed away
from sun by the solar wind

<u>What makes nucleus?</u>   MS-Bookshelf

nucleus is made of ice and frozen gases and
    some heavier substances
surrounding that is a much larger coma—it is
    made up of gases

<u>What makes nucleus?</u>   MS-Bookshelf

nucleus = ice + slush/ maybe rocky in very
center—scientists not sure

To turn these five note cards into paragraphs, we need to
weave their contents together in an interesting way. There's no
right way and no wrong way. Read the cards a few times until
they begin to fit together well in your mind.

We could put all this information into one or two paragraphs, but three seemed good to us. See what you think. (Keep in mind that these paragraphs have been buffed and polished. Don't try to get yours perfect on the first pass!)

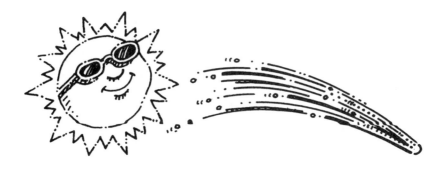

Some people call comets "dirty snowballs" because they are essentially frozen dirt. They are made up of water, carbon dioxide, ammonia, methane, grit, and dust—all frozen together.

The center of the comet (called the nucleus) is made of ice, frozen gases, and slush. Some scientists believe that there is rocky material at the very center, but no one is sure of that. Surrounding the nucleus is a much larger area called the coma, which is made up of gases.

The tail of a comet is made of gas and dust particles. It always points away from the sun because the gases and particles are pushed away from the sun by the solar wind.

Here are the note cards you wrote for Key Idea B (How big are comets?) while you were doing your research:

What's the diameter?   MS-Bookshelf

up to 1.5 million miles in diameter

What's the diameter?	Grolier CD
about 80,000 miles in diameter	

How long is tail?	MS-Bookshelf
tail grows longer when it's closer to the sun	

How long is tail?	MS-Bookshelf
tail can be 100 million miles long	

These four note cards seem to fit well into one paragraph.

Comets look small to us, but they are huge. Scientists estimate that they are from 80,000 miles in diameter to 1.5 million miles in diameter. The part that looks biggest

to us is the tail, which can be 100 million miles long!
The tail is longest when the comet is closest to the sun.

Here are the note cards you wrote about Key Idea C (How
do comets travel? Where do they go?) while you were doing
the research:

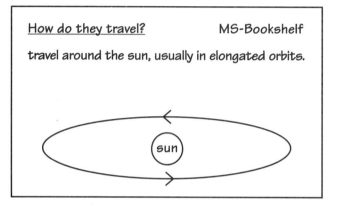

How do they travel?   MS-Bookshelf

travel around the sun, usually in elongated orbits.

How do they travel?   MS-Bookshelf

go faster when closer to the sun

How do they travel?   MS-Bookshelf

farther away from Earth than the moon is
they stay in orbit a long time, nobody is sure
   how long

How close to Earth?   MS-Bookshelf

The closest one in the past 200 years was
    2.9 million miles from Earth in 1983.

How often seen?   MS-Bookshelf

about 10 new ones are discovered every
    year—better and better telescopes
one is visible without a telescope about every
    three years

When do we see one?   MS-Bookshelf

We can see it only when it is fairly close to
    the sun.

Here is how these note cards might turn into paragraphs:

Comets travel around the sun, and they usually travel in a
path like a long, flat oval instead of a circle. The closer
the comet is to the sun, the faster it moves. Also, the closer
it is to the sun, the easier it is for us on Earth to see.

Comets orbit the sun for a long time, but nobody is sure how long. Because we have increasingly more advanced telescopes, about ten new comets are discovered every year. About one comet every three years is bright enough for us to see without a telescope.

Although they sometimes seem to be very close to us, comets are farther away than the moon. In the past 200 years, the closest one to Earth was 2.9 million miles away. That was in 1983.

Tip

Think of your note cards as pieces of a puzzle: "Maybe this card would fit well next to that one. No, it seems better there. Yep, that looks just right." Play with your note cards in your mind until several seem to fit. That's how good paragraphs are born—ideas that fit smoothly together like pieces of a jigsaw puzzle.

Guidelines for good paragraphs

Have one clear main idea

Ask yourself what the main idea of the paragraph is, then stick with that idea all the way through the paragraph. Otherwise, you'll end up with a mushy paragraph.

MUSHY:

The ancient pyramids were sort of like buildings but now they are tourist attractions. They were burial places. Their kings were called pharaohs in Egypt. Lots of stones were used and mummies were there. Lots of stuff was there, too. (Good grief, what is the main idea here?)

CLEAR:

The ancient stone pyramids of Egypt were built as tombs for the pharaohs (kings). Over two million blocks of stone were used to build the pyramid at Giza, burial place of the pharaoh Khufu. Inside the burial chamber, the pharaoh's body was preserved like that of other mummies: wrapped tightly in specially prepared cloths and placed in a stone casket. His family placed food, clothes, jewels, and weapons around him, believing he might need these in the next world.

(The main idea here is clear: The pyramids were tombs for the kings.)

With each new idea, start a new paragraph

TOO MANY IDEAS IN ONE PARAGRAPH:

Spiders build webs to catch their prey. Some spiders build shapeless webs. Other spiders build elaborately beautiful webs. The shapeless types of webs have trip wires built into them. The spider hides nearby. An insect lands on the web and stumbles over the trip wire. Before it knows what has happened, the spider runs out of hiding and grabs its lunch. The more elaborate webs that you often see outdoors suspended between shrubs or trees are sticky. Insects literally get "glued" to the web. As they struggle, the web wiggles and the spider is alerted that dinner has arrived. Some tropical spiders build webs so huge that they can trap small birds.

BETTER:

(Notice that in order to break this into three clearer paragraphs, some reorganizing and rewriting was needed.)

Spiders build webs to catch their prey. Most webs are designed to catch insects, although some tropical spiders build webs so huge that they can trap small birds!

Some spiders build shapeless webs. These types of webs have trip wires built into them. The spider hides nearby. An insect lands on the web and stumbles over the trip wire. Before the insect knows what has happened, the spider runs out of hiding and grabs its lunch.

Other spiders build elaborately beautiful webs. You often see these outdoors suspended between shrubs or trees. These webs are sticky, and insects literally get "glued" to the web. As they struggle, the web wiggles and the spider is alerted that dinner has arrived.

(Notice in each of these three paragraphs that there's one main idea and several supporting ideas.)

A paragraph (usually) is more than one sentence

Unless you have a dynamite idea that you want to highlight, don't write paragraphs with only one sentence.

TOO SHORT:
> One-sentence paragraphs usually look too short.

BETTER:
> One-sentence paragraphs are usually not a good idea. Unless you have one powerful idea or a knock'-em-dead sentence that you want to highlight, one-sentence paragraphs usually look too simple, even silly. Put several sentences about the same idea together to create a successful paragraph—just like this one!

SUCCESSFUL CONCLUSIONS

Have you ever been to a movie that was exciting right up to the last fifteen minutes and then was confusing, boring, or ridiculous? That's very frustrating, isn't it? After putting lots of work into making your paper sizzle, don't let the ending fizzle.

How can you pack your last paragraph (your conclusion) with power? Here are some techniques that work:

Repeat the main idea of your project

INTRODUCTION:

Several million years ago (give or take a millennium or two), the world looked very different than it does now. Earth's continents were not where they now are. North America and Europe were joined. South America and Africa were side-by-side, too.

(A millennium, by the way, is 1,000 years.)

WEAK CONCLUSION:

As we've seen, the continents of Earth have shifted over millions of years and maps are different because places are in different places, and future maps might be different, too, if things keep moving around like they have been.

STRONGER CONCLUSION:

Scientists have uncovered lots of evidence that the continents haven't always been where they now are. They have moved, and they are still moving. Change is slow. It may take thousands or millions of years, but who knows—maybe someday California will be cozy with Japan, or maybe Australia will be in our backyards. (Notice this conclusion has the same light-hearted tone of the introduction. If the introduction were more serious, you would want to write a more serious conclusion.)

Give an example or tell a very short story that sums up your main idea

INTRODUCTION:

Most pilots avoid flying near violent storms; others fly straight into them. Hurricane hunters are airplanes specially designed to fly through hurricanes in order to gather information that might save the lives of people on the ground.

WEAK CONCLUSION:

Hurricane hunter airplanes do a lot for research and public safety, and we should be glad because of them.

STRONGER CONCLUSION:

As B. J. Styron climbs into her specially designed hurricane hunter airplane, she knows she will fly straight into weather that any other pilot would avoid. She will encounter wind so strong it would knock a lesser pilot right out of the sky. She will face danger in the sky for the sake of research—and for the safety of those on the ground.

Make a prediction based on what you learned in your research

INTRODUCTION:

> Robots are not just characters in science fiction movies. They are very useful helpers in many aspects of American science and industry, and more are being introduced every day.

WEAK CONCLUSION:

> Some robots are already used in American science and I predict there will be more use of them as time goes on.

STRONGER CONCLUSION:

> Robots already clean swimming pools, perform welding tasks in car assembly lines, and guide surgeons' scalpels in complicated surgery. Many scientists predict that by the year 2020, tiny robots will be able to travel through the human body detecting disease, that robots will be driving our cars, and that our homes will have robots performing many ordinary chores. Robots will become as much a part of our everyday lives as television is today.

Use words that connect back to words in your introduction

INTRODUCTION:

> When it comes to communication, porpoises lead the underwater pack.

WEAK CONCLUSION:

> I hope I've shown that porpoises are good communicators.

STRONGER CONCLUSION:

> They may not have telephones or email, but we shouldn't underestimate their abilities to communicate. Porpoises have the most sophisticated and most fascinating communication skills in the sea.

Sum up your thesis (if you have one)

Leave your reader feeling that you have done what you said you were going to do—you have proven or supported your thesis.

THE TOPIC OF THE PAPER:

forest fires

THE THESIS OF THE PAPER:

Although forest fires can do a lot of damage, they are a very important part of nature's way of keeping the planet healthy.

WEAK CONCLUSION:

People should appreciate forest fires because they aren't all bad.

(This is an opinion, but it doesn't do anything to prove the thesis.)

STRONGER CONCLUSION:

Forest fires clean the forest of debris, allow seeds to germinate that cannot germinate without fire, and create habitats for certain types of plants and animals. Although they can cause costly tragedies for humans, there is no question that forest fires are a vital part of nature's system for keeping the planet alive, balanced, and healthy.

CURES FOR WRITER'S BLOCK

All writers get stuck sometimes and experience what's called "writer's block." It feels just like it sounds—like your brain ran into a concrete block and won't budge. You feel as if your fingers completely forgot how to write or type, and that blank piece of paper or empty computer screen seems to get bigger . . . and blanker.

When you crash into the writer's block, don't panic. It happens to every writer now and then. Thank goodness, it doesn't last. Writer's block can happen for many different reasons, and there are many helpful solutions. Here are some ideas:

PROBLEM:

You get embarrassed and shy as you write. You are thinking, "Why would anybody want to read what I have to say?"

CURE:

Pretend you're writing a letter to your best friend, your grandmother, or anyone you like and trust. Tell him or her what you discovered in your research as if it were a story. Relax and enjoy telling this person your special story.

PROBLEM:

You realize you don't have some of the facts you need and you keep running back and forth to the library, the Internet, or your reference books.

CURE:

Keep writing even if you don't know all the facts. Jot notes to yourself about what you need to look up later. You might write something like this: Bengal tigers usually weigh about ____ pounds. You can fill in the blank later.

PROBLEM:

You're trying to write when you're exhausted.

CURE:

Take a nap. There's nothing harder than trying to write when your brain is screaming, "Let me sleep!" Don't put off your work until the last minute; all good writers need breaks.

PROBLEM:

You're bored with this project because you've been working on it too long.

CURE:

It's just like eating nothing for five days but pizza with pepperoni and extra olives—you get sick and tired of it.

Put down your project for a day or two. When you come back to it, your project will look a lot more interesting. If your deadline is too close to do this, shoot a few baskets, take a short bike ride, or do some cart wheels to clear your head and energize your body.

PROBLEM:

You're bored with this project because you're not interested in it and haven't been interested in it from the start.

CURE:

Sometimes you have to do research on topics that don't seem particularly interesting to you. Play creative mind games with yourself to make the project feel important. Pretend you're writing to the school principal or even to the president. Pretend that you need to convince him or her why your ideas are important because your ideas, if you present them well, could make a big difference to all the students in your school. (Some day your ideas just might make a big difference to a lot of people, so think of this project as practice for something important you'll do later in your life.)

PROBLEM:

You're trying to make your first draft perfect.

CURE:

Now is the time to get a bunch of words down on paper. Don't worry about spotless spelling and perfect punctuation. Make a mess—you can clean it up later. Just write.

PROBLEM:

You're confused about how to write one part of the paper or how to explain one particular idea.

CURE:

Don't let that tricky section slow you down. Keep writing. Go to another section of the paper and come back to the troublesome part later. There's no law that says you have to finish part one before you work on part two. (Some professional writers write the last paragraph first. That way they know where they're headed.)

PROBLEM:

A mean, bully voice is jabbering inside your mind saying things like, "That last sentence was really dumb. Got any more stupid ideas?" and, "Your friends will make fun of you when you read that in class." You feel terrible and want to give up.

CURE:

Ornery, critical, bully voices are part of many creative projects. All of us are sometimes afraid that we can't do the job well enough. That's normal. Just don't let the bully in your mind stop you! Be mean right back and tell the bully to hush. Then give yourself an A+ for courage. Creative projects take courage because nobody else has ever done this exact project before. You're doing it in your own way and expressing your own ideas. That's sometimes a little scary—but it's also very exciting.

BRAIN TICKLERS
Set #12

1. Krista is doing a paper about the possibility that humans will colonize outer space. Here is her topic with her main idea:

TOPIC:
space colonization
MAIN IDEA:
Modern technology is advancing in ways that will make space colonization a very real possibility by the year 2050.

Krista has written the following three introductions, and now it's time to select one. She asks your advice on which one to choose. What would you tell her about each of these introductions?

INTRODUCTION 1:
Will people go into space? A lot of people have wanted to. Science fiction stories talk about it all the time. There are lots of stories about people being in space, but we're not all the way there yet.

INTRODUCTION 2:
People can't live in outer space unless they have equipment that can handle it. Equipment is being developed that might make it possible to live in outer space. Space colonization means living for a while in space, and good equipment made by scientists is needed.

INTRODUCTION 3:
There have been many science fiction movies about humans colonizing outer space. Will Hollywood's fantasy ever be real? It's possible. This paper will explore how far technology has come and how far it needs to go before people can be at home in outer space.

2. Brian is researching the beginning days of America's most popular sports. Here are the note cards he made about the history of basketball:

Bball first began   MS-Bookshelf

James Naismith taught physical education at the YMCA Training School in Springfield, Mass.

Bball first began   MS-Bookshelf

he devised a game he called basketball in December 1891

---

the rules   MS-Bookshelf

Naismith came up with 13 rules, all of which are still in effect today

---

other stuff   MS-Bookshelf

Naismith eventually became a physician

How was it played?   MS-Bookshelf

Naismith hung up two peach baskets, one at
either end of the gym

How was it played?   MS-Bookshelf

the first ball used was a soccer ball; players
threw it back and forth until one team was
able to throw it into a basket

<u>history of the game</u>   MS-Bookshelf

became popular extremely quickly; was played a lot in YMCA gyms on the east coast

---

<u>history of the game</u>   MS-Bookshelf

the first metal hoop—1893
the first backboard—1895

<u>history of the game</u>   MS-Bookshelf

first men's intercollegiate game—1897
first professional league—1898

<u>history of the game</u>   MS-Bookshelf

popular all over the U.S. by the 1920s

Brian took these note cards and wrote four different paragraphs. Which of these paragraphs is good? How could Brian improve the others?

PARAGRAPH 1:

James Naismith taught gym in Massachusetts. He later became a doctor. He invented basketball. They hung peach baskets up and used soccer balls. The game became popular really fast and the first backboard was invented in 1895.

PARAGRAPH 2:

James Naismith, inventor of basketball, hung up two peach baskets as goals. The first metal hoop was introduced in 1893, and basketball became very popular quickly after that.

PARAGRAPH 3:

James Naismith taught physical education at the YMCA Training School in Springfield, Massachusetts. He devised a game he called basketball in December 1891. Naismith came up with 13 rules, all of which are still in effect today. He later became a doctor. He hung up two peach baskets, one at either end of the gym. The first ball used was a soccer ball; players threw it back and forth until one team was able to throw it into a basket. The game became popular very quickly and was played a lot in YMCA gyms on the east coast. The first metal hoop was introduced in 1893, the first backboard in 1895. The first men's intercollegiate game was played in 1897 and the first professional league was formed in 1898. The game was popular all over the U.S. by the 1920s.

PARAGRAPH 4:

Before becoming a doctor, James Naismith taught physical education at the YMCA Training School in Springfield, Massachusetts. In December, 1891, he devised a game that he called basketball. He hung up two peach baskets, one at either end of the school gym, and players threw a soccer ball back and forth until one team threw it into a basket. The 13 rules Naismith devised for the game are still in effect today. Basketball became popular extremely quickly and was played a lot in YMCA gyms on the east coast. The first metal hoop was introduced in 1893, and the first professional league was formed in 1898. By the 1920s, only 30 years after the very first point was scored in a peach basket, basketball was being played all over the U.S.

3. Was Christopher Columbus really the first person to discover America? Rick is interested in that question. He has written these three paragraphs for his report and asks you to edit them. What would you tell him?

PARAGRAPH 1:

Before Christopher Columbus came to America, other European explorers went places looking for stuff. Leif Eriksson did it, too. He got blown off course during a trip he was taking and maybe came to America somewhere, but nobody is sure about where. Then another guy from where Eriksson was from sailed later to some of those places, too.

PARAGRAPH 2:

Long before Christopher Columbus came to America, other European seafarers may have made contact with the New World. According to Norse sagas, Leif Eriksson sailed to a place he called Vinland around the year 1000. Nobody is positive, but that could have been either Nova Scotia or New England. The legend says that Eriksson was blown off course during a trip from Norway to Greenland. In the year 1010, Thorfinn Karlsefni set out from Iceland to settle in the area of North America that Eriksson had discovered. Historians disagree about exactly where he traveled and how long he stayed, but after a while Karlsefni left that part of the world and sailed to Greenland.

PARAGRAPH 3:

Long before Christopher Columbus came to America, other European seafarers may have made contact with the New World. According to Norse sagas, Leif Eriksson sailed to a place he called Vinland around the year 1000. Nobody is positive, but that could have been either Nova Scotia or New England. The legend says that Eriksson was blown off course during a trip from Norway to Greenland. Norway's economy was energized by the discovery of oil in the North Sea during the 1960s.

4. Carmen is doing a paper about life on Mars. Here are her topic and her introductory paragraph:

TOPIC:

Is there life on Mars?

INTRODUCTION:

For thousands of years, people have wondered if there is life on other planets. In recent years, our advanced technology has allowed us to view Mars up close. On July 20, 1976, Viking I (an unmanned probe) landed on Mars. It was the first manmade object to visit another planet. In July 1997, the unmanned Pathfinder journeyed to Mars. One of the big questions of both missions was "is there life here?"

What do you think about each of these conclusions?

CONCLUSION 1:

So there probably isn't any life on Mars.

CONCLUSION 2:

Modern science has confirmed that there are, in fact, no little green people on Mars. There are no purple people or pink ones either. Perhaps there was life there millions of years ago (no one knows for sure), but there isn't anybody home these days.

CONCLUSION 3:

Life on other planets has been questioned for many years and will continue to be the subject of fantasy and debate. Maybe we are alone in the universe, maybe not. Poets and scholars continue to wonder, as do the makers of sci-fi movies. It is a fascinating question, and one that is not likely to be answered for many years, if ever. Are we alone? We may never know.

CONCLUSION 4:

Both Viking I and Pathfinder searched for evidence of life on Mars, but none was found. At this point, research has shown that there is no life on Mars, but the whole story may not yet be known. Some scientists urge expeditions to search for fossils, which would indicate that life did exist there long ago. If fossils were found, they might hold information about a fascinating ancient history on our sister planet, and we humans might have to rethink our belief that we are alone in this solar system.

(Answers on page 182.)

BRAIN TICKLERS— THE ANSWERS

Set #11, page 150

1. If Justin were telling a story he wouldn't talk about the happy-ever-after ending before saying "once upon a time." In this case, Justin has written about Chicago being rebuilt before writing about the fire. These ideas work much better in chronological order:

   1. Chicago before the fire
   2. How a cow kicked over a lantern in a barn to start the fire
   3. How long the fire raged
   4. The extent of the destruction
   5. Rebuilding the city of Chicago

2. Julie skipped a very important step. Even though her treasure hunt led her to some very interesting information, she didn't organize her note cards. That means she didn't organize her thoughts. Julie doesn't like to organize stuff, so she skipped this step. That's sad, because after all that great research, Julie could end up thinking she's not a good writer—all because she didn't take time to organize her super research into clear ideas.

Set #12, page 173

1. Krista did a great job by writing three different introductions. Now you can help her pick the very best one.

    INTRODUCTION 1:

    This introduction is unfocused and a little confusing. There is no clear statement of the paper's main idea. First, plenty of people have already been in space as astronauts. Krista needs to be clear that she is talking about space colonization, not just "being in space." Second, this paper is not about science fiction stories; it's about modern scientific technology, and Krista hasn't mentioned that at all.

    INTRODUCTION 2:

    Krista was probably distracted when she wrote this introduction. Her topic is exciting, but this introduction is boring. A little more pizzazz in her writing would let the reader feel how exciting this topic is.

    INTRODUCTION 3:

    Now that's a super introduction. It's very clear, lets the reader know exactly what she's going to be talking about, and makes the reader want to know more. Krista's off to a great start.

2. Brian took some super notes. Now let's help him select a super paragraph.

    PARAGRAPH 1:

    These sentences are choppy. Combining ideas and making the sentences a little longer would help.

    PARAGRAPH 2:

    A lot of interesting and important information has been left out of this paragraph.

    PARAGRAPH 3:

    Notice that Brian simply took the note cards one after another and made sentences out of them. He didn't try to weave the information together in a smooth or interesting way. Although this paragraph isn't bad, notice how much better Paragraph 4 is.

PARAGRAPH 4:

Good job, Brian. Now that's a great paragraph! All the ideas weave together very nicely. Although two pieces of information are left out (the first backboard and the first men's intercollegiate game), they aren't necessary for the paragraph to be complete.

3. Let's look at the three paragraphs Rick wrote.

PARAGRAPH 1:

Uh-oh, this paragraph is very mushy. What's the point? What is Rick trying to say?

PARAGRAPH 2:

This is not bad, but it would read better as two paragraphs. The first half talks about Leif Eriksson and the second half talks about Thorfinn Karlsefni. It would read better if a new paragraph began with the sentence "In the year 1010 . . ."

PARAGRAPH 3:

What is that last sentence doing there? It doesn't have anything to do with the other ideas and information. If Rick deletes the last sentence, this paragraph is fine.

4. Carmen wants some advice on what she wrote.

CONCLUSION 1:

Sorry, Carmen, this is a very dull ending . . . yawn.

CONCLUSION 2:

This might be fine if Carmen's introduction were extremely light-hearted. But it's not, so the conclusion should be more serious.

CONCLUSION 3:

This is good writing, but it doesn't connect with the main idea. The main idea is about scientists determining if there is life on Mars. This conclusion is about life in general in outer space, and it is much more philosophical than scientific in tone.

CONCLUSION 4:

Now Carmen's cooking! That's a good conclusion.

CHAPTER SEVEN

Buff and Shine Your Treasure

If a diver found a chest of treasure at the bottom of the sea, that treasure might not look so beautiful at first. With a little polishing, though, the treasure could really sparkle. Writing is like that. Your first draft might not shine, but with a little clean-up, it will.

If possible, put your paper down for a day or two. Time away from your writing gives you fresh eyes, and fresh eyes can see mistakes and improvements much better than tired eyes. This is another good reason to get started on your project early, rather than waiting until the last minute.

EDITING TOOLS

Here are four very helpful friends to have beside you when you go over your paper:

Dictionary

If you shoot a ball through a basket, how do you spell the game you're playing? Is it "basketball" or "basket ball"? Is a cool beat spelled "ryhthm" or "rhythm"? If people emigrate, does that mean they leave the country or enter the country? Dictionaries were written because nobody can remember the definitions and spelling of every single word in the English language.

Thesaurus

If you've used the word *big* so many times that your paper looks small, find another word. A thesaurus can suggest great alternatives. How about *monstrous* or *gigantic* or *colossal?*

Use a dictionary to make sure the word you've chosen has the exact meaning you want. If you describe Godzilla as a monstrous reptile instead of a big reptile, you've added some zest to your writing. But if you describe your mother as having a monstrous heart, she might be offended. Used in this context, the word *monstrous* seems to imply that she has the heart of a monster rather than that she has a big heart.

Let the thesaurus help you choose words that are sharp, clear, and expressive, but don't try to impress your reader with how many big words you can use. An extended queue of erudite or sophisticated verbiage gives your text the semblance of elitism or preposterousness. (Translation: A long string of fancy words makes your writing look snobby or silly.)

Grammar and punctuation handbook

Should I put a colon or a comma here? Should I use *who* or *whom?* Nobody remembers all the rules all the time. Having a handbook handy makes your editing job much easier.

Red pen

When you edit your rough draft, use a red pen. Flamingo pink or Halloween orange are also fine—any color that shows up so brightly that you can easily see what changes you need to make.

EDITING YOUR PAPER

When you pick up your paper after a day or two of rest, it's almost as if you're reading it for the first time. Pretend that you know little or nothing about this subject. As you read your paper, does it make sense to someone who is unfamiliar with the topic? Some writers like to read each paragraph aloud. Sometimes when you hear the words out loud it's easier to tell whether they make sense.

If possible (and if it's okay with your teacher), have someone else read your paper. Ask them which parts are confusing or unclear, then rework those paragraphs.

Here are a few things to look for when you revise your paper:

Title

Is the title interesting or boring? Does it give a clear idea of what the paper is going to be about?

Introduction

Is the introduction clear or muddy? Does it let the reader know exactly what the report is going to be about? Is it written in a way that makes the reader want to know more?

Flow of ideas

Do the paragraphs flow smoothly or do the ideas sound jumbled and out of order?

Amount of information

Is there enough information (enough facts) in this report or does it leave the reader frustrated because there's too little information? Is there too much information? Have you thrown in unrelated facts that confuse your reader? How would your paper sound if you cut out those parts?

Conclusion

Is the conclusion strong or does it fizzle out?

Check your spelling

When it comes to spelling, English is not an easy language. Spelling goofs happen all the time! We are professional writers and we've never written a paper without a single spelling mistake to correct—especially in the rough draft.

There are three ways to check your spelling. Your best bet is to use all three:

Dictionary

If there is any word you're not 100 percent sure how to spell, look it up in the dictionary.

Editor

Have someone else proofread your paper and circle spelling mistakes with red ink.

Spell checker

Type on a word processor and use a spell checker. Just remember that the computer doesn't know when you mean to write "wood" and when you mean to write "would." Tea computer wood nut sea any think wrung wiz dish sentence, sew bee care full an dabble chick yore composter's spilling!

Check your punctuation, grammar, and writing style

Here are some very common punctuation goofs. Check your paper carefully for these:

- comma splices (using a comma to separate two complete sentences)
- incorrect punctuation of parentheses
- incorrect punctuation of quotations
- incorrect use of colons and semicolons

Here are some very common grammar goofs. Check your paper carefully for these:

- run-on sentences
- incomplete sentences (sentence fragments)
- verbs not agreeing with their subjects
- pronouns not agreeing with their antecedents

Here are some very common writing-style goofs. Check your paper carefully for these:

- padding a paper with unnecessary words and redundant phrases
- unclear, unfocused sentences and paragraphs
- clumsy, awkwardly written sentences
- informal, slangy words and phrases when formal English is better

Make it clean and neat

As long as you turn in your paper on time, it doesn't matter how it looks, right? Wrong! Would you prefer to watch your favorite television show on an eight-inch screen that frizzles and frazzles or on a thirty-inch screen that has a sharp, clear picture? Would your teacher rather see a neat, clean paper or a mess?

Go back over all the guidelines your teacher gave you. Double check that you've followed any rules your teacher specified about cover sheets, bibliographies, footnotes, graphics, drawings, line spacing, and margins. If your teacher did not give you guidelines about any of these things, here are some suggestions for producing clean, neat projects:

Use notebook-size (8¹/₂" x 11") paper

Using gigantic paper or tiny paper is okay if you are creating a huge display poster or a newspaper for elves.

Leave margins

Whether you're using a computer or writing by hand, don't write all the way to the edge of the paper. Leave one inch of white space all the way around the paper.

Indent each paragraph or skip an extra space between paragraphs

Otherwise, it is hard to tell where one paragraph stops and another begins.

Use only one side of the paper

That makes your teacher's job of reading your paper much easier.

Double space—unless your teacher tells you otherwise

If you're writing by hand, that means skip every other line. It is much easier to read things that are doublespaced, and "easier to read" almost always means a better grade.

Put your last name and a page number on each page

Use small letters at the bottom of each page. That might look like this: McCall, page 3. If the staples come out or your binder falls off, your teacher will know how to put your paper back together.

Hook your pages together

Use staples, a thin notebook, or any of the types of covers that are available in office supply stores. Imagine that your teacher drives home with the car windows down. Do you want your paper to be the one that flies apart—with some pages floating out the window?

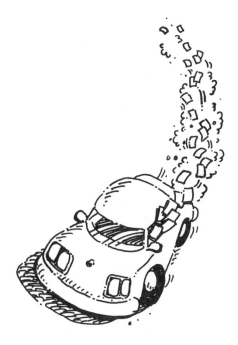

Use blue or black ink if you write your paper by hand

Don't use pencils, ink in flaming chartreuse, or pens that write in rainbow colors.

Write neatly

Make your letters large enough that your teacher can easily read your handwriting.

Use a simple font if you write on a computer

Don't use funky fonts except in titles. **THIS KIND OF FONT** is easy to read only in very small doses. *Even though this font is pretty, try to read it for five pages and you'll go bonkers.*

MAPS AND ILLUSTRATIONS

Be smart: Don't spend so much time on fancy maps or drawings that you don't have time for the really important parts of
research—finding facts and organizing them into clear
thoughts. If you do include graphics in your project, here are
some good ways to get the material you need:

- **Cut pictures** from a magazine (but only if it is *your*
  magazine), brochure, greeting card, catalog, etc. Of
  course you should never cut from a magazine, newspaper, or book in the library.

- **Photocopy** pictures from a magazine or book.

- **Trace** maps from an atlas.

- **Buy post cards.** They are inexpensive and often have
  wonderful photography of animals, geography, and art.

- **Use clip art** if you have access to a computer and clip
  art on disk or CD-ROM.

- **Download** pictures from the Internet.

- **Scan** photographs into your computer, incorporate them
  into your paper, and print the artwork along with your
  words.

- **Take photographs** yourself. Be sure to allow time for
  them to be developed.

- **Draw graphics** by hand or on your computer using a
  drawing program.

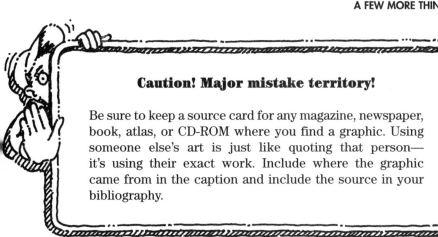

Caution! Major mistake territory!

Be sure to keep a source card for any magazine, newspaper, book, atlas, or CD-ROM where you find a graphic. Using someone else's art is just like quoting that person—it's using their exact work. Include where the graphic came from in the caption and include the source in your bibliography.

A FEW MORE THINGS TO CHECK

Quotations

Make sure you put all direct quotations (places where you used another writer's exact words) in quotation marks and tell whose words they are.

Titles and labels

Are there titles or labels for all the pictures, maps, or graphics?

Bibliography

Have you included a bibliography (and footnotes if required) and carefully proofread for errors? Have you typed it in accordance with the style sheet your teacher gave you or the one presented in this book (it's in Appendix B on page 225)?

Backups

Always keep a copy of what you give your teacher. You can do that by photocopying your paper or keeping a backup on a computer. What if your teacher's brother, a famous magazine editor, came over to his sister's house for dinner, saw your paper on her coffee table, read it, loved it, without thinking tucked it into his pocket (forgeting to tell his sister, of course), finished dessert, and went home? What are you going to do when your teacher says she can't find your paper?

CHAPTER EIGHT

A Sample Research Report

CHOOSING A TOPIC

Josh's assignment is to write a report between three and five pages long, and he is free to pick any topic. After thinking about what he'd like to research, he remembers a movie he saw a while back about the funny adventures of a youngster living in the White House. He decides he wants to find out what it's like to live in the White House.

He settles on the topic "Children in the White House." Now that he has an idea, he uses this checklist to make sure it's a good idea:

Getting an idea for a topic

✔	The topic is not too big.
✔	The topic is not too small.
✔	The topic is not too easy.
✔	Information won't be too hard to understand.
✔	Information won't be too hard to find.
✔	The topic is not too dull or boring.
N/A	The thesis (if you need one) is clear.

(Note: See Appendix A on page 219 for checklists you can photocopy and fill out for your projects.)

This topic is not too big as long as Josh doesn't try to write everything about every kid who ever lived in the White House. It's not too small and not too easy, and the information won't be hard to find or understand. Also, if he uses the right sources, it's not a boring topic. Since this is a report, Josh doesn't need a thesis; he'll just be describing a little bit about kids who have lived in the White House. (The note N/A in the checklist means it's Not Applicable to this project.)

Next, Josh needs to be sure he knows what the teacher expects. Here's a checklist:

Knowing what the teacher wants

✔	Topic is on-track with the approach the teacher expects
3–5 pp	Length the paper should be
May 1	Deadline for the final project
N/A	Deadline for any intermediate steps: outline, note cards, rough draft, etc.
4	Number of sources the teacher expects
1	How many general encyclopedias may you use?
books	Do specialized encyclopedias count as books or as encyclopedias?
N/A	Other stuff needed: costumes, materials for posters, etc.
any ok	Guidelines for writing: by hand? typewriter? computer?
N/A	Guidelines for pictures, maps, drawings, diagrams

Next, Josh asks questions about his topic. If he doesn't know enough about the topic to know what questions to ask, he could read an article in a magazine, newspaper, or encyclopedia to get some ideas. How many kids have lived in the White House? Which presidents had kids? What were the kids' lives like? Here's a checklist for this part of the work:

Asking questions about your topic

> ✔   Brain doodle; gather some preliminary information about the topic: magazines, talks with experts, encyclopedias, etc.
> ✔   Make a list of questions about your topic.
> ✔   Organize the questions into key ideas. (This is your search plan.)

For the paper on kids in the White House, Josh comes up with these key ideas:

1. Who are the kids who have lived in the White House?
2. What was life like for them in the White House?
3. What are some unusual or unique facts about their experiences in the White House?

Where would you think Josh could find information about this topic? Here's another checklist to use:

Looking for information—what would be useful sources for this project?

✔	General encyclopedias
✔	CD-ROM encyclopedias
✔	Specialized encyclopedias
	Atlases, yearbooks, almanacs, directories, dictionaries, biographical references, and indexes
✔	Books
✔	Newspapers
✔	Magazines
✔	Magazines and newspapers on CD-ROM (SIRS, InfoTrac, etc.)
	Other types of CD-ROMs (maps, books of quotations, etc.)
✔	Videos and movies
	Audiotapes
	Music recordings
	Odds and ends in the library (vertical files and artifacts)
	Interviews
	Questionnaires
✔	Internet
	Local Chamber of Commerce
	Local historical society
	Museums
	Historic sites
	Travel agencies; state or national tourist offices
	Government agencies
	Businesses
	Journals of professional organizations
	Television shows
	Radio shows
	Newsletters
	Public service organizations

The best places to look for information for this report are probably books, newspaper articles, magazine articles, and the Internet. Josh doesn't personally know any presidents' kids, so it wouldn't be easy to get an interview. It is certainly possible to find information in other places, but the ones with check-marks are good places to start.

Next, Josh takes a little time to get organized before he starts his research. That way he's sure not to get behind. Here's a checklist to use:

Getting organized

4 wks	How much time do you have before the project is due?
no	Do you need to write for information? Do that early.
yes	Will you need a computer? printer? Internet access?
no	Do you need to set up meetings with team members?
no	Do you need to set up interviews?
no	Do you need to set up trips to museums or special libraries?
no	Do you need to buy materials for models, maps, posters, etc.?

Josh goes to his school library to look for good sources of information and does a computer search for books, magazine articles, and newspaper articles about White House kids. He finds a book titled *White House Children* written by Miriam Anne Bourne and several relevant articles in *The World Book Encyclopedia*. He finds an article in a magazine, and he even discovers a White House homepage for kids on the Internet.

Josh makes source cards for each of his sources. Here's the one for the book by Bourne:

> **Source card for a book with one author**
>
> | | |
> |---|---|
> | Author | Bourne, Miriam Anne |
> | Title of book | White House Children |
> | City where published | New York |
> | Name of publisher | Random House |
> | Year published | 1979 |

Taking notes is not about copying words. Josh carefully reads what the author has written, then puts that idea on a note card in his own words. Here are two examples of his notes:

TEXT IN BOURNE'S BOOK:

> "What if your father or grandmother or uncle became President? Would you like to leave home for Washington, D.C.? Would you like to move into the White House?
> "That is what Presidents' families have been doing since 1800. Before that there was no White House. There was not even a Washington, D.C."

JOSH'S NOTE CARD:

<u>early years</u>   Bourne, 8

Since 1800, presidents have lived in the White House with their families.

TEXT IN *THE WORLD BOOK ENCYCLOPEDIA:*

"Johnson's two attractive daughters added youthful zest to the White House. Luci liked to invite friends to teenage dances in the Blue Room. Lynda often cornered her father's visitors to ask them about current affairs. Mrs. Johnson tried to keep life normal for her daughters, but this was sometimes impossible. For example, Secret Service agents had to accompany the girls on their dates."

JOSH'S NOTE CARD:

<u>early years</u>   World Book 1997
                                              vol J-K, page 144

President and Mrs. Johnson had two attractive daughters, Luci and Lynda. The girls sometimes had their friends over for teen-age dance parties in the Blue Room of the White House. When Luci and Lynda went on dates, the Secret Service would go along.

Here's the checklist to use during the note-taking phase of the research:

Taking notes

_____✔_____ Make a source card for each source you read.

_____yes_____ Are your notes in your own words?

_____✔_____ Write the main idea on each card.

_____✔_____ If you copy anything, put quotation marks around those words.

_____✔_____ Write on each note card where that information came from (source and page number).

_____✔_____ Be sure to look up information in enough different sources.

When all the notes are taken, it's time for Josh to organize his note cards and write the rough draft of the paper. Here are two checklists to help with those tasks:

Organizing your note cards

_____✔_____ Put your note cards into stacks of key ideas.

_____✔_____ Put a label on each key idea stack.

_____✔_____ Arrange the key idea stacks in an order that tells your story well and makes clear sense. Would any of these orders work well?

    _____✔_____ chronological order

    _____ question–answer

    _____ similarities–differences

    _____ for–against

    _____ problems–solutions

_____✔_____ Take each key idea stack, one at a time, and arrange the cards within the stack in an order that is clear.

_____✔_____ Look over any extra, wait-and-see cards. Do they fit into any of your key ideas? Do any of them fit together to make a new key idea?

Writing the rough draft of the paper

✔ Think about what the main idea of your project is and write an introduction. Be clear and focused. Would one of these styles work well?

    _____ Ask a question.

    _____ Use words to draw an interesting picture.

    _____ Tell a short story.

    ✔ Tell an interesting or shocking fact.

    _____ Make a strong-muscled statement of the main idea.

✔ Take the first key idea stack of cards and turn your note cards into paragraphs. Do this for each key idea stack.

✔ Check your paragraphs for these mistakes:

    _____ not clear what the idea of the paragraph is

    _____ too long, too much information

    _____ too short, not enough information

    _____ too rambling, too many different main ideas

✔ Write a strong, clear conclusion. Consider these styles:

    ✔ Repeat the main idea of the project.

    _____ Give an example or tell a short story that sums up the main idea.

    _____ Make a prediction.

    _____ Use words that connect back to words in the introduction.

    _____ Sum up your thesis (if there is one).

Here's Josh's paper about White House kids.

White House Kids

The public has always been curious about the lives of kids in the White House. In 1996, the Walt Disney movie "First Kid" took a funny look at the everyday life of a child in the White House. Today, there is even a site on the Internet where people can get information about what it's really like to be the nation's "First Kid."

The presidents of the United States have lived in the White House with their families since 1800. John Adams, who was the second president (1797–1801), lived there while it was being built. His granddaughter, Susanna Adams, was the first child to live in the White House.

When Abraham Lincoln was the 16th president (1861–65), his sons Willie and Tad played war games in the White House. They also rode ponies, popped corn, and played leap frog with their father while living there.

Josh Zinn, page 1

The oldest Lincoln son, Robert, was away at school while his father was president. For their schooling, Willie and Tad had a tutor. Mrs. Lincoln set up desks and a blackboard in the State Dining Room so that they would have a place to study.

The younger Lincoln boys sometimes got into trouble. One time Tad tied together all the cords that rang bells used to call the servants. He pulled all the cords at the same time and all the servants came running. Another time, Tad and Willie tied two pet goats to a kitchen chair then led them into the parlor where Mrs. Lincoln was giving a tea party. All the guests were very surprised!

Later, tragedy struck the Lincoln family. Willie got sick and died. After that, Tad spent a lot of time with his father. President Lincoln took Tad to visit army camps during the Civil War, and Tad helped cheer up the troops.

Theodore Roosevelt (the 26th president, 1901–1909) moved into the White House with six children (Quentin, 3;

Josh Zinn, page 2

Archie, 7; Ethel, 10; Kermit, 12; Ted, 14; and Alice, 17)
and lots of pets. Among the family's animals were dogs,
guinea pigs, turtles, hens, rabbits, ponies, snakes, a
parrot, and a horned toad.

After a while, Archie and Quentin were the only kids
living at home. They rollerskated, bicycled, walked on
stilts, and played hide-and-seek. They even slid down the
stairs in the White House on trays. Sometimes the president
would wrestle and have pillow fights with the boys.

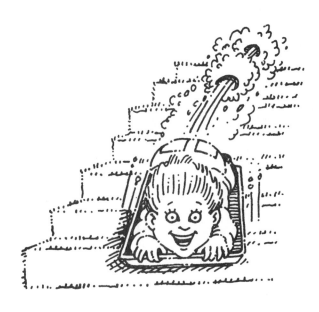

Josh Zinn, page 3

John Kennedy's children were the talk of the nation when he was the 35th president (1961–63). When President Kennedy and his wife Jacqueline came into the White House, Caroline was three years old and John Jr. was two months old. They were the youngest children to live in the White House in more than 60 years.

There were many stories about the children in the newspapers. People were amused by Caroline's cute comments. "John-John," as the Kennedys called their son, was written about in the newspapers when he started to crawl and when he first stood.

For play times, the Kennedy kids had swings, a sandbox and a trampoline on the White House lawn. Caroline loved horses. Her mother put her on a pony when she was 18 months old. At five years old she rode her pony Macaroni in a show and won a blue ribbon.

Since Kennedy's presidency, all the children living in the White House have been girls. Lyndon Johnson (the

Josh Zinn, page 4

36th president, 1963–69) had two attractive daughters,

Luci and Lynda. They would invite friends to teenage

dance parties in the Blue Room of the White House. When

they went on dates, the Secret Service would go along.

When Jimmy Carter became the 39th president

(1977–81), his daughter Amy was nine years old. She

walked with her father and mother during the parade to

the White House on inauguration day. Part of the way,

Amy skipped.

While she lived in the White House, Amy took violin

lessons. She had a cat named Misty-Melarky Ying-Yang

Carter. When Amy's grown-up brothers came to visit the

White House with their families, they all would play table

tennis and chess, bowl in the White House bowling alley,

swim in the White House pool, and watch movies in the

White House theater.

When Bill Clinton was elected 42nd president and

was getting ready to move into the White House with his

Josh Zinn, page 5

family in 1993, this is what the magazine *Scholastic Update* said about his daughter, Chelsea Clinton: "By most accounts, Chelsea leads an ordinary life. Her parents don't let her go to R-rated movies; they'll decide if she may have her ears pierced after she turns 13. She wears braces, plays volleyball and softball, hangs out at the mall, and talks on the phone for hours. Someday, she hopes to be an astronautical engineer."

During her years in the White House, Chelsea enjoyed playing soccer and practicing ballet. Her favorite subjects in school were math and foreign languages.

Here are some interesting facts about other White House kids:

- Esther Cleveland, the daughter of Grover Cleveland (the 22nd and 24th president, 1885–89 and 1893–97), was the only child to be born in the White House.

Josh Zinn, page 6

- Charlie Taft, the son of William Taft (the 27th president, 1909–13), once asked to work the telephone switchboard in the White House.

- David, Barbara Anne, Mary Jean, and Susan—the grandchildren of Dwight Eisenhower (the 34th president, 1953–61)—drove battery-powered cars in the driveway when they came to the White House to visit their grandparents.

- John Tyler (the 10th president, 1841–45) had the most children—15 of them – living in the White House.

From 1800, when John Adams's granddaughter moved into the White House, until Chelsea Clinton left home for college in 1997, children have often been part of life around the White House. It will be very interesting to see who's the next First Kid.

Josh Zinn, page 7

This draft of the White House kids paper is not very rough. It's been polished a time or two. But it's always a good idea to go over your paper very carefully looking for ways to make it sparkle and shine. Here is a checklist to help you remember what to look for.

Editing and cleaning up the paper

yes	Is the title interesting and clear?
yes	Is the introduction interesting and clear?
yes	Do the paragraphs flow smoothly?
yes	Is there enough information given?
_no_	Is there too much unrelated information thrown in?
strong	Is the conclusion strong or does it fizzle out?
✔	Check spelling.
✔	Check punctuation, grammar, and writing style.
yes	Does the paper look clean and neat?
✔	Use notebook-size paper.
✔	Use only one side of the paper.
✔	Leave one-inch margins.
N/A	If you write by hand, use blue or black ink.
✔	Indent paragraphs or leave a space between paragraphs.
✔	Double space.
✔	Check that handwriting (or computer font) is easy to read.
✔	Put your name and a page number on each page.
✔	Hook the pages together.
yes	Are all quotations in quotation marks?
N/A	Are pictures, maps, and graphics labeled?
_no_	Do you need to include footnotes or endnotes?

____✔____ Check that your bibliography is
written in correct MLA style or a
style approved by your teacher.
___no___ Do you need a special type of cover
sheet or title page?
___yes___ Do you have a backup copy of your
paper before you turn it in?

WRITING THE BIBLIOGRAPHY

When someone helps you out with a problem, you say thank
you, right? The people who help you with your research
include the people who wrote the books, articles, maps,
pamphlets, CD-ROMs, and charts that gave you all the useful
information for your project. Think of the bibliography as a
way of saying thank you to all those people.

The bibliography comes at the end of your paper. It is an
alphabetized list of all your sources—articles you read, books
you used, interviews with experts, Internet addresses, and
every other place you found information for your project.

There are several styles for bibliographies. Sometimes
your teacher will give you a particular style he wants you to
use. If he doesn't, you can't go wrong using the style you see
here. We use the MLA (Modern Language Association) style
throughout this book; it is one of the most commonly used
and widely accepted styles.

Here is what Josh's bibliography looks like:

BIBLIOGRAPHY FOR "WHITE HOUSE KIDS"

Bourne, Miriam Anne. *White House Children.* New York: Random House, 1979.

"Cleveland, Grover." *The World Book Encyclopedia.* 1997 ed.

"Coolidge, Calvin." *The World Book Encyclopedia.* 1997 ed.

First Kid. Prod. Roger Birnbaum. Walt Disney Pictures Video, 1996.

"Johnson, Lyndon Baines." *The World Book Encyclopedia.* 1997 ed.

"Kennedy, John Fitzgerald." *The World Book Encyclopedia.* 1997 ed.

Monagle, K. "America's First Kid." *Scholastic Update* 15 Jan. 1993: 15.

"Roosevelt, Franklin Delano." *The World Book Encyclopedia.* 1997 ed.

"Welcome to the White House for Kids." http://www.whitehouse.gov/WH/kids/html/home.html (Retrieved 16 July 1997).

Notice that the entries in a bibliography are in alphabetical order. The words *a, an,* and *the* don't count, so ignore those when you're alphabetizing your list of sources. Also, alphabetize by the author's last name, not his or her first name. If there is no author, alphabetize by the title of the article, film, pamphlet, etc.

When you do your first bibliography it may seem like there are just too many rules to remember. It's true, there are many details that need to be exact—a comma there, no comma there, a period there, no period there, and things like that. If you want to drive yourself crazy, try to memorize how to write bibliographies. If you have more fun things to do, don't memorize. Just find a "recipe" that shows you a correct style and use it. In Appendix B we give you "recipes" for many different types of sources.

APPENDIX A
PAINLESS CHECKLISTS

Getting an idea for a topic

_____ The topic is not too big.
_____ The topic is not too small.
_____ The topic is not too easy.
_____ Information won't be too hard to understand.
_____ Information won't be too hard to find.
_____ The topic is not too dull or boring.
_____ The thesis (if you need one) is clear.

Knowing what the teacher wants

_____ Topic is on-track with the approach the teacher expects
_____ Length the paper should be
_____ Deadline for the final project
_____ Deadline for any intermediate steps: outline, note cards, rough draft, etc.
_____ Number of sources the teacher expects
_____ How many general encyclopedias may you use?
_____ Do specialized encyclopedias count as books or as encyclopedias?
_____ Other stuff needed: costumes, materials for posters, etc.
_____ Guidelines for writing: by hand? typewriter? computer?
_____ Guidelines for pictures, maps, drawings, diagrams

Asking questions about your topic

_____ Brain doodle—gather some preliminary information about the topic: magazines, talks with experts, encyclopedias, etc.

_____ Make a list of questions about your topic.

_____ Organize the questions into key ideas. (This is your search plan.)

Looking for information—what would be useful sources?

_____ General encyclopedias

_____ CD-ROM encyclopedias

_____ Specialized encyclopedias

_____ Atlases, yearbooks, almanacs, directories, dictionaries, biographical references, and indexes

_____ Books

_____ Newspapers

_____ Magazines

_____ Magazines and newspapers on CD-ROM (SIRS, InfoTrac, etc.)

_____ Other types of CD-ROMs (maps, books of quotations, etc.)

_____ Videos and movies

_____ Audio tapes

_____ Music recordings

_____ Odds and ends in the library (vertical files and artifacts)

_____ Interviews

_____ Questionnaires

_____ Internet

_____ Local Chamber of Commerce

_____ Local historical society

_____ Museums

_____ Historic sites

_____ Travel agencies; state or national tourist offices

_____ Government agencies
_____ Businesses
_____ Journals of professional organizations
_____ Television shows
_____ Radio shows
_____ Newsletters
_____ Public service organizations

Getting organized

_____ How much time do you have before the project is due?
_____ Do you need to write for information? Do that early.
_____ Will you need a computer? printer? Internet access?
_____ Do you need to set up meetings with team members?
_____ Do you need to set up interviews?
_____ Do you need to set up trips to museums or special libraries?
_____ Do you need to buy materials for models, maps, posters, etc.?

Taking notes

_____ Make a source card for each source you read.
_____ Are your notes in your own words?
_____ Write the main idea on each card.
_____ If you copy anything, put quotation marks around those words.
_____ Write on each note card where that information came from (source and page number).
_____ Be sure to look up information in enough different sources.

Organizing your note cards

_____ Put your note cards into stacks of key ideas.

_____ Put a label on each key idea stack.

_____ Arrange the key idea stacks in an order that tells your story well and makes clear sense. Would any of these orders work well?

      _____ chronological order

      _____ question-answer

      _____ similarities-differences

      _____ for-against

      _____ problems-solutions

_____ Take each key idea stack, one at a time, and arrange the cards within the stack in an order that is clear.

_____ Look over any extra, wait-and-see cards. Do they fit into any of your key ideas? Do any of them fit together to make a new key idea?

Writing the rough draft of the paper

_____ Think about what the main idea of your project is and write an introduction. Be clear and focused. Would one of these styles work well?

       _____ Ask a question.

       _____ Use words to draw an interesting picture.

       _____ Tell a short story.

       _____ Tell an interesting or shocking fact.

       _____ Make a strong-muscled statement of the main idea.

_____ Take the first key idea stack of cards and turn your note cards into paragraphs. Do this for each key idea stack.

_____ Check your paragraphs for these mistakes:

       _____ not clear what the idea of the paragraph is

       _____ too long, too much information

       _____ too short, not enough information

       _____ too rambling, too many different main ideas

_____ Write a strong, clear conclusion. Consider these styles:

       _____ Repeat the main idea of the project.

       _____ Give an example or tell a short story that sums up the main idea.

       _____ Make a prediction.

       _____ Use words that connect back to words in the introduction.

       _____ Sum up your thesis (if there is one).

Editing and cleaning up the paper

_____ Is the title interesting and clear?

_____ Is the introduction interesting and clear?

_____ Do the paragraphs flow smoothly?

_____ Is there enough information given?

_____ Is there too much unrelated information thrown in?

_____ Is the conclusion strong or does it fizzle out?

_____ Check spelling.

_____ Check punctuation, grammar, and writing style.

_____ Does the paper look clean and neat?

> _____ Use notebook-size paper.
>
> _____ Use only one side of the paper.
>
> _____ Leave one-inch margins.
>
> _____ If you write by hand, use blue or black ink.
>
> _____ Indent paragraphs or leave a space between paragraphs.
>
> _____ Doublespace.
>
> _____ Check that handwriting (or computer font) is easy to read.
>
> _____ Put your name and a page number on each page.
>
> _____ Hook the pages together.

_____ Are all quotations in quotation marks?

_____ Are pictures, maps, and graphics labeled?

_____ Do you need to include footnotes or endnotes?

_____ Check that your bibliography is written in correct MLA style or a style approved by your teacher.

_____ Do you need a special type of cover sheet or title page?

_____ Do you have a backup copy of your paper before you turn it in?

APPENDIX B
BIBLIOGRAPHIES
AND SOURCE CARDS

What exactly is a bibliography? You already know that a *biography* is information about a person. Well, a *bibliography* is information about books. (*Biblio* is from the Greek word *biblion*, meaning book.) When you do research, you need to tell people about the books and other sources in which you found information. You do that by writing a bibliography.

There are several ways to write bibliographies and present information about your sources. In this book we show the style used by the Modern Language Association (MLA). This is a widely accepted style that you'll probably use through high school and later in your research projects. If your teacher doesn't require a different style, you can't go wrong using the MLA style.

Bibliographies are like the "Simon says" games that little kids play. Everything has to be done just so—every piece of punctuation must be consistent. Simon says put magazine articles in quotation marks (not underlining), and Simon says put book titles in underlining or italics (not quotation marks). The rules are very picky and very difficult to memorize.

However, doing your bibliography can be painless. If you use the source cards in this appendix, you won't have to memorize the rules. Just fill in the blanks and follow the example at the bottom of each card showing what punctuation to use in your bibliography (what words to capitalize, where to put periods and commas, where to use a colon, etc.). If you are writing on a computer, you can use italics anywhere these cards show underlining (in fact, italics are preferable), but that's the *only* thing that is okay to change.

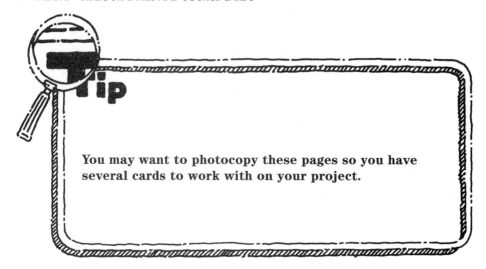

You may want to photocopy these pages so you have several cards to work with on your project.

By the way, all the titles in this appendix are made up. Some of these might sound like fun things to read, but exist only in our minds, not in any libraries.

Reference book articles with no author given

(encyclopedias, yearbooks, almanacs, etc.)

> Source card for a reference book article with no author given
>
> Title of article _____
>
> Reference book _____
>
> Year of edition (ed.) _____
>
> How to cite this in your bibliography:
>
> "Yellow-Bellied Aardvarks." Encyclopedia Animalia. 1997 ed.

Reference book articles with an author

Source card for a reference book article with an author

Author　　　　　　　　_____

Title of article　　　　_____

Reference book　　　　_____

Year of edition (ed.)　_____

How to cite this in your bibliography:

Yew, P. "Skunks." <u>Encyclopedia Animalia</u>. 1995 ed.

CD-ROM encyclopedia articles

Source card for a CD-ROM encyclopedia article

Author (if given)　　　_____
Title of article　　　　_____
Name of CD-ROM　　　_____
Year of edition (ed.)　_____
City where published　_____
Name of publisher　　_____
Year published　　　　_____

How to cite this in your bibliography:

Slurp, Susie. "Table Manners." <u>My Old Bookshelf</u>. 1995–96 ed. CD-ROM. Chicago: Software for Kids, Inc., 1996.

Magazine articles

Source card for a magazine article

Author　　　　　　　_____
Title of article　　　　_____
Magazine　　　　　　_____
Date (mo. yr for a monthly magazine; day mo. yr for a weekly magazine)　_____
Page numbers　　　　_____

How to cite this in your bibliography:

Elliott, Meg. "The Gerbil Ate My Homework." <u>The Magazine of Animal Antics</u> Sep. 1996: 36–39.

Newspaper articles

Source card for a newspaper article

Author (if given) _____
Title of article _____
Newspaper _____
Date (day mo. yr) _____
Section and page _____

How to cite this in your bibliography:

Rescue, Randy. "Ice Packs on the Head Prevent
Research Project Distress among Middle School
Students." Daily Newsworthy News 10 Jan. 1998: D7.

Cartoons

Source card for a cartoon

Cartoonist's name _____
Title of cartoon _____
Name of publisher _____
City _____
Date (day mo. yr) _____
Page _____

How to cite this in your bibliography:

Taylor, Floyd. "Barney and Andy." Cartoon. The Sentinel
[Mayberry, NC] 29 Aug. 1997: 8D.

Books or pamphlets with one author

Source card for a book or pamphlet with one author

Author _____
Title of book _____
City where published _____
Name of publisher _____
Year published _____

How to cite this in your bibliography:

Zinn, Joshua. Tennis with No Strings Attached.
Hilton Head, SC: Yellow Ball Press, 1996.

Books or pamphlets with two authors

Source card for a book or pamphlet with two authors

Authors _____
Title of book _____
City where published _____
Name of publisher _____
Year published _____

How to cite this in your bibliography:

Lewis, Meriwether, and William Clark. <u>Our Famous Cross-Country Trip</u>. Columbia, OR: Wild West Press, 1822.

Interviews

Source card for a personal interview

Interviewee _____
Type of interview _____
   (telephone, mail, email, or personal)
Date of interview _____
   (day mo. yr)

How to cite this in your bibliography:

Lyon, Cynthia. Personal interview. 17 Dec. 1997.

Films

Source card for a film

Title _____
Producer or director _____
Main performers _____
Distributor (studio) _____
Year produced _____

How to cite this in your bibliography:

<u>The Great Research Project Adventure</u>. Dir. John E. Student. With Tom Cruise, Arnold Schwarzenegger, and Julia Roberts. Eagle's Nest Studio, 1997.

(You don't have to include the stars in the film.)

Television programs

> Source card for a television program
>
> Title   _____
> Producer or director   _____
> Show   _____
> Network or station   _____
> Date (day mo. yr)   _____
>
> How to cite this in your bibliography:
>
> <u>Modern Sports Heroes</u>. Prod. Muscles Malone. PBS
> Special. KABC, Chicago. 6 Sept. 1996.

If you can't find some of this information, don't worry. Just use whatever information you have.

Internet sites

> Source card for an Internet site
>
> Author (if given)   _____
> Title of article (if given)   _____
> Title of the site   _____
> Document date (if given)   _____
> Internet address   _____
> Date you logged on   _____
> (day mo. yr)
>
> How to cite this in your bibliography:
>
> Rabbit, Brer. "Food for Thought." <u>Home Page for Small,
> Furry Animals</u>. 1997. http://www.hares/~bunnies.com
> (Retrieved 3 Oct. 1997).

Online databases such as America Online

Source card for an online database

Author (if given) _____
Title of article _____
Date (if given) _____
Title of database _____
Name of computer service _____
Date you logged on _____

How to cite this in your bibliography:

Elliott, Kate. "Interactive Horseback Riding." 16 Nov. 1984. <u>Horse News Yearbook</u>. Online. Kids Online. 12 Sep. 1997.

Periodical CD-ROM databases such as SIRS and InfoTrac

Source card for a CD-ROM database

Author (if given) _____
Title of article _____
Original publisher _____
Date published _____
Section or pages _____
Title of the CD-ROM _____
Publisher of CD-ROM _____
   (if relevant)
Date CD-ROM published

How to cite this in your bibliography:

Matthews, Michael. "Basketbail in Antarctica." <u>Hoops News</u> Feb. 1996: 46–47. <u>Sports Abstracts</u>. CD-ROM. SportSoft, Inc. 1996.

Government publications

Source card for a government publication

Name of the government_____
   (state, county, country, etc.)
Name of the agency _____
Title of the publication _____
City where published _____
Name of publisher _____
Year published

How to cite this in your bibliography:

United States. Dept. of Education. <u>A Report on the Feasibility of Making Saturday a School Day</u>. Washington: Government Printing Office, 1996.

There are many other types of sources you might need to list in your bibliography. Ask your librarian or teacher if you need a reference book showing you how to cite any of these sources or any others not shown here:

- a book translated from another language
- a book by a corporate author (written by a company)
- an edited compilation of chapters by separate authors
- music in printed form (sheet music)
- music recorded on records, audiotapes, or CDs
- live theater performances: operas, plays, ballets, etc.
- computer manuals
- computer software

APPENDIX C
INTERNET ADDRESSES

Astronomy and Space

NASA Homepage
http://www.nasa.gov/

- NASA's news of the day
- history of NASA
- links to information about specific NASA missions
- links to "Women of NASA," a K-12 wind tunnel program, K-12 science programs, and "Aviation Science Careers and Opportunities"

Ames Space Archive: Pretty Pictures
http://www.stsci.edu/astroweb/yp_pictures.html

- a link site that takes you to pictures from outer space
- links to more than 100 pages ranging from "Ames Space Archive" to "Virtual Trips to Black Holes and Neutron Stars"

Welcome to the Planets
http://pds.jpl.nasa.gov/planets/

- a collection of some of the best pictures from NASA's planetary exploration program
- pictures of each of the nine planets in our solar system along with profiles giving the diameter of each planet, distance from sun, length of the year, and more
- glossary of astronomy terms
- links to related sites

Mars Pathfinder
http://mpfwww.jpl.nasa.gov/default.html

- pictures and description of the Pathfinder mission to Mars
- "Bird's Eye View of the Landing Site"
- analysis of soil samples taken at the site
- daily online live chat about the mission
- descriptions of upcoming NASA missions

Kid's Space
http://liftoff.msfc.nasa.gov/kids/

- a site for younger kids
- calculate how much you would weigh on the moon
- print out pages and color them in
- puzzles, scrambled pictures, and animated stories
- kids' quiz

Starchild: A Learning Center for Young Astronomers
http://starchild.gsfc.nasa.gov/

- two levels of explanation (younger kids and older kids) of the solar system and the universe
- glossary of astronomical terms
- sections on astronauts, space wardrobes, space travel, space probes, and the Hubble space telescope

Windows to the Universe
http://www.windows.umich.edu/

- information and pictures of our planet, solar system, and universe
- myths about the universe
- space missions
- three levels (beginner, intermediate, advanced) of tours and questions
- ask a scientist your questions about the universe

Physical Sciences

Chem 4 Kids!
http://www.chem4kids.com/

- a site about chemistry
- the properties of matter and the nature of atoms
- includes the Periodic Table of Elements
- a glossary of chemistry terms
- take a chemistry quiz
- famous and important chemists

Iowa State University Entomology Image Gallery
http://www.ent.iastate.edu/imagegallery/

- a site about insects
- information about beetles, butterflies and moths; cicadas and leafhoppers; flies and mosquitoes; grasshoppers and crickets; lice, mites, ticks, and true bugs (stink bugs)
- thumbnail previews (small pictures) of the different bugs with links to larger images

Missouri Botanical Garden: Just for Kids
http://www.mobot.org/mbgnet/justkids.htm

- a site about botany (plants)
- pictures and descriptions of rivers, streams, and other aquatic habitats
- virtual plant habitats: deserts, grasslands, temperate forests, jungle rain forests, tundra, Alaskan taiga (an evergreen forest south of the tundra)
- "Report from the Tundra"—meeting Eskimo kids and touring this area of Alaska
- "Flying into the Bush"—flying a single-engine airplane into the Alaskan taiga
- "Desert Journey through Israel"—visiting the ancient land to see where three plant habitats (biomes) meet
- a map that shows endangered plant species in all 50 states

The Field Museum Online
http://www.fmnh.org/Home.htm

- a site about paleontology (the study of ancient plants and animals using fossils)
- illustrations of dinosaurs
- animations of a sabertooth cat running, a Triceratops running, and a Moropus eating
- interactive games—what if dinosaurs had survived?
- hear music made with mammoth bones

Digital Learning Center for Microbial Ecology
http://commtechlab.msu.edu/CTLProjects/dlc-me/

- a site about microscopic organisms
- "Microbe Zoo"—images and descriptions of microscopic organisms and the habitats in which they live
- microbes in the news—stories from newspapers and magazines
- profiles of microbiologists
- "The Curious Microbe"—tales of amazing microbes and their curious environments

The Franklin Institute Science Museum Online
http://www.fi.edu/tfi/welcome.html

- search the museum's archives for information on science topics such as meteorology, physics, botany, and much more
- several virtual museum tours with text, graphics, animation, video, and sound

The American Museum of Natural History Fossil Halls
http://www.amnh.org/Exhibition/Fossil_Halls

- a virtual exhibit of dinosaurs and other fossils
- timeline, dates, and descriptions of periods (with pictures)—Pleistocene, Cretaceous, Jurassic, Devonian, etc.
- links to vertebrate evolution, exhibitions, and people

Biology and Animal Sciences

Electronic Zoo Animal Information
http://www.exploratorium.edu/learning_studio/sciencesites.html

- quickly search the entire Web for information about amphibians, birds, cats, dogs, ferrets, fish, horses, invertebrates, marine mammals, pigs, primates, reptiles, rabbits, rodents, wild animals, zoo animals, even fictional animals

The Animal Omnibus (Birmingham Zoo)
http://www.birminghamzoo.com/ao/

- hundreds of links to other sites devoted to specific animals
- includes a very helpful index—amphibians, arthropods, birds, dinosaurs, fishes, mammals, mollusks, and reptiles

ZooNet—All about Zoos
http://www.mindspring.com/~zoonet/

- links to zoo homepages
- index to zoos in the United States and throughout the world
- links to pictures and descriptions of specific animals, including some endangered species

The Interactive Frog Dissection: An Online Tutorial
http://curry.edschool.Virginia.EDU/go/frog/

- descriptions, pictures, and video images on the procedures for dissecting frogs
- takes you through the steps of preparation, skin incisions, muscle incisions, and identification of internal organs

Human Anatomy On-Line
http://www.innerbody.com/htm/sysselec.html

- click on the ten anatomy systems for more detail about each system
- includes images, descriptions, and animations
- search for parts of the anatomy

DNA: The Instruction Manual for All Life
http://www.thetech.org/hyper/genome/

- what DNA is and how it affects you
- zoom in on a human hand until you get to the nucleus of a cell where DNA is examined

Earth Sciences

Earthquakes: What's Shakin'?
http://www.thetech.org/hyper/Earthquakes/intro/

- illustrations and descriptions of earthquake science including seismographs, plate tectonics, faults, and waves
- earthquake history and safety
- a ten-second video of a classroom during a 1989 earthquake in California

Volcano World
http://volcano.und.nodak.edu/

- volcano images and information
- a list of currently active volcanoes with links to pictures of several volcanoes throughout the world
- a description of the latest eruptions
- volcanoes on other planets
- volcanic parks and monuments
- volcano video clips
- ask a volcanologist a question of your own

Hurricane: Storm Science
http://www.miamisci.org/hurricane/

- weather conditions inside a hurricane
- pictures and descriptions of "hurricane hunter" airplanes that fly into the center of the storms to collect information
- how to make a hurricane weather station of your own
- safety—a shopping list of things to have before a hurricane strikes

PSC (Plymouth State College) Meteorology Program Cloud Boutique
http://vortex.plymouth.edu/clouds.html

- pictures and descriptions of basic cloud forms
- link to the "University of Illinois Cloud Catalog"

Oceans

The Oceanic Research Group: Wonders of the Seas
http://www.oceanicresearch.org/lesson.html

- pictures and descriptions of undersea life
- sponges, cnidarians, mollusks, and more
- send questions to the Oceanic Research Group

<u>Florida Aquarium</u>
http://www.sptimes.com/aquarium/default.html

- photos of various undersea creatures
- information about habitats—mangrove forests, bays and beaches, coral reefs, and more
- wade around in the "Swamp of Knowledge"
- test your knowledge with "CritterMatch"
- "The Story of a Drop of Water"

<u>The E-Quarium (Monterey Bay Aquarium)</u>
http://www.mbayaq.org/

- computer tour of the Monterey Bay, going from rocky tide pools to a large underwater canyon
- pictures and descriptions of an undersea forest of towering kelp that is home to tiny turban snails and huge amber kelp crabs
- information about the aquarium's conservation efforts and programs in marine research

<u>Underwater World (Monterey Bay Aquarium)</u>
http://www.pathfinder.com/@@UEVUjwQAsxgzn97W/ pathfinder/kidstuff/underwater/

- "Lost in a Forgotten Sea"—a virtual adventure to various underwater habitats all over the world
- "Freaky Fishes Family Album"—pictures of unusual-looking undersea animals
- "Fishy questions" (undersea trivia)—how deep in the ocean can fish live, how many different kinds of fish are there, what are the biggest fish in the world?

<u>FINS: Fish Information Service</u>
http://www.actwin.com/fish/index.cgi

- information about aquariums and aquarium-related topics
- catalog of marine fish and freshwater fish with information, common and scientific names, and pictures
- aquatic plants
- do-it-yourself aquarium projects
- links to other fish sites

Math

Ask Dr. Math
http://forum.swarthmore.edu/dr.math/

- submit questions to Dr. Math (actually a group of more than 150 volunteers from around the world) by sending email; answers are sent back to you by email
- a searchable archive organized by grade level and topic
- "Frequently Asked Questions"—includes prime numbers, pi, the golden ratio, and Pascal's triangle

Frequently Asked Questions in Mathematics
http://daisy.uwaterloo.ca:80/~alopez-o/math-faq/math-faq.html

- find answers to nagging math questions
- What are numbers?
- What's the largest known prime number?
- Why is there no Nobel Prize in mathematics?
- play math games

Literature and the Arts

The WebMuseum
http://sunsite.unc.edu/louvre/

- a set of over 100 works of art by Paul Cezanne
- famous paintings by 200 other artists with short biographies of each
- glossary of terms describing painting styles

The Complete Works of William Shakespeare
http://the-tech.mit.edu/Shakespeare/works.html

- full text of Shakespeare's works
- search for words and phrases
- includes a discussion area, "Bartlett's Familiar Shakespearean Quotations," and a glossary
- links to other Shakespeare resources on the Internet

ARTSEDGE
http://artsedge.kennedy-center.org/srp.html

- links to sites helpful for projects about the arts
- arts of Africa, China, India, Japan, Australia, Latin America, Peru
- arts of Native American Indians
- arts of colonial America
- American arts of the 1920s, 1930s, 1940s

Yahooligans Classical Music
http://www.yahooligans.com/Entertainment/Music/Classical/

- a link site for kids about classical music

History

Gateway to World History
http://www.hartford-hwp.com/gateway/

- a wide variety of links to sites on the history of the world
- includes search engines to find Internet resources on specific topics, images from history, documents, and maps

The Museum of Antiquities
http://www.ncl.ac.uk/~nantiq/

- a site about ancient history
- the evolutionary stages of life since the creation of Earth
- how human activities and technology have changed in the past 2 million years
- "Flints and Stones"—how people lived in Europe during the Late Stone Age
- misunderstandings about the lives of Stone Age peoples

The Middle Ages: Feudal Life
http://www.learner.org/exhibits/middleages/feudal.html

- what life was like in the Middle Ages
- health, arts and entertainment, clothing, homes, religion
- good links to related sites

The Forum Romanum—Exploring an Ancient Market Place
http://library.advanced.org/11402/

- a brief history of Rome
- what life was like in ancient Rome
- the forum, religion, daily life, biographies

National Museum of American History
http://www.si.edu/organiza/museums/nmah/

- timeline of important events in American history
- links to pages with information about particular eras

An Outline of American History: The War of Independence
http://odur.let.rug.nl/~usa/H/1990/chap2.htm

- thirteen pages each describing a phase of the American revolution
- from "Frontier Fosters Self-Reliance" to "Colonies Gain Victory and Freedom"
- links to pages such as the Declaration of Independence
- links to biographies of notable people such as Lafayette and Benjamin Franklin

A Brief History of the Civil War
http://www.dartmouth.edu/~civilwar/

- pictures and descriptions of the Civil War
- links to pages with more information about important people and battles

The American Civil War Homepage
http://sunsite.utk.edu/civil-war

- information about individual battles and many other facets of the war
- links to the most useful sites about the Civil War
- links to maps, images, and flags

Biographical Profiles of Some Important 19th-Century African Americans
http://www.brightmoments.com/blackhistory/index.html#people

- Frederick Douglass, Harriet Tubman, Nat Turner, Sojurner Truth, and others
- multiple-choice history quiz about African Americans

Smithsonian: American Social and Cultural History
http://www.si.edu/resource/faq/nmah/culture.htm

- American social and cultural history
- musical history
- political history
- Native American Indians
- African American resources
- Hispanic/Latino resources
- Asian American resources

The Learning Page of the Library of Congress
http://lcweb2.loc.gov/ammem/ndlpedu/index.html

- search for information in the American Memory collections, which contain documents, motion pictures, photographs, and sound recordings that are important in American history
- search by events, people, places, time and topics (one page has a list of suggested topics)
- "Touring Turn-of-the-Century America"
- "America's First Look into the Camera: Daguerreotypes"
- "Evolution of the Conservation Movement"

Geography

The 50 States of the United States: Capital Cities and Information Links
http://www.scvol.com/States/

- a list of states with maps and information about each state's government
- for each state—the state bird, tree, flag, flower and song as well as information on state parks, newspapers, and population

The World Factbook
http://www.odci.gov/cia/publications/nsolo/wfb-all.htm

- almanaclike information about every country in the world
- information about the Arctic, Atlantic, Indian, and Pacific oceans

National Geographic Map Machine
http://www.nationalgeographic.com/resources/ngo/maps/

- information on cartography (mapmaking)
- glossary of geographic terms
- "The Map Machine Atlas"—maps, flags, facts, and profiles for the countries of the world and the United States
- links to sites with map libraries

Mapmaker, Mapmaker, Make Me a Map
http://loki.ur.utk.edu/ut2Kids/maps/map.html

- a playful but informative site that tells you how maps are made
- definitions of many terms—"equal-area," "conformal," "azimuthal equidistant," etc.
- download a geography crossword puzzle
- links to other geography sites on the Web

Destination: Himalayas—Where Earth Meets Sky
http://library.advanced.org/10131/

- Himalayan lands (from India to Nepal)
- geology of the area
- trekking, flora and fauna, environmental problems, maps

Social Studies and Government

Welcome to the White House
http://www.whitehouse.gov/WH/Welcome.html

- information about the president and vice president, their accomplishments, and their families
- send email to the president and vice president
- the history of the White House with pictures
- search White House documents and listen to speeches
- "The White House for Kids"—the executive branch of our government from a kid's-eye view

U.S. House of Representatives
http://www.house.gov

- directory of all House members and their staffs
- legislation currently before this branch of Congress
- list of House of Representatives organizations, task forces, and commissions

U.S. Senate
http://www.senate.gov/

- information on senators
- recent legislative actions
- Senate history, procedures, and terminology

FedWorld's Supreme Court Decisions Homepage
http://www.fedworld.gov/supcourt/index.htm

- over 7,000 Supreme Court opinions from 1937 through 1975
- link to a site with 300 of the most historic decisions
- link to a site with all of the court's decisions since 1990

Legi-Slate
http://www.legislate.com/ldinside.htm

- read the text of the great documents on which our government is based
- step-by-step explanation of how Congress turns a bill into law
- definitions of terms used by the government
- list of members of U.S. Congress and how to contact them
- legislation introduced each week
- "Today in Congress"—visit a web page of *The Washington Post* to view the daily schedules for various legislative committees

United States Treasury's Page for Kids
http://www.ustreas.gov/treasury/kids/

- information about the U.S. monetary system
- browse or search the historic treasury collection
- get answers to frequently asked questions—What states are shown on the back of the five-dollar bill? How much paper currency does the Treasury Department print every day?
- biographical information about past treasury secretaries
- facts about the gold bullion depository at Fort Knox, KY
- important dates in treasury history

Current Events

CNN Interactive
http://www.cnn.com

- text and pictures of world news, U.S. news, and local news
- weather, sports, science and technology, travel, health, politics, and other features
- search the site for current events facts
- download news clips from the video vault
- take a news quiz

The Nando Times
http://www2.nando.net/

- text and pictures of news, politics, business, and entertainment, business, opinions
- check out "Today's Photos"
- search the site for recent events in the news

USA Today Online Database
http://167.8.29.8/plweb-cgi/ixacct.pl

- search the site for stories from "USA Today Online News" for the past six days
- search for *very* current events: the database is updated every hour

Mercury Center NewsLibrary
http://newslibrary.infi.net/sj/

- searchable archive containing nearly 1 million articles published in 25 newspapers across the United States
- free list of headlines and the first paragraph of each story in your search
- $1 charge each time you download the full text of an archived story

Reference

Kids Web Reference Material

http://www.npac.syr.edu/textbook/kidsweb/reference.html

- Acronym Dictionary (FBI, CIA, NATO, AIDS, and other abbreviations)
- American English Dictionary
- Bartlett's Familiar Quotations
- Biographical Dictionary
- Online Dictionary of Computing
- Roget's Thesaurus
- U.S. Census Information (1990)
- Webster's Dictionary
- World Factbook

My Virtual Reference Desk

http://www.refdesk.com/

- like being in the reference room of a huge library
- dictionaries
- several different online encyclopedias
- atlases
- *Who's Who*
- newspapers from the United States and around the world
- books of quotations
- thesaurus
- links to the Atomic Clock and other neat sites

The Internet Public Library
http://www.ipl.org/ref/CenterNG.html

- guide to over 700 homepages of organizations and associations
- Native American authors
- presidents of the United States: biographies, speeches and writings, election results, odd facts
- facts and information about the American states
- online newspapers from around the world—searchable by region and title
- online magazines—searchable by subject and title
- many books
- link to the Internet Public Library's Teen Collection—resources of interest to teenagers

Other Cool Sites

Coasters.Net
http://www.coasters.net/

- roller coasters and amusement parks around the world
- roller coaster designers
- links to other roller coaster pages

U.S. Olympics Committee Online
http://www.olympic-usa.org/

- events, athletes, plans for upcoming games

Sport! Science@The Exploratorium
http://www.exploratorium.edu/sports/index.html

- in the science of cycling, learn about the aerodynamics of wheels, the techniques of frame making, and how to calculate braking distances
- learn about the physics involved in rock climbing and in bouncing balls
- check out sport science links
- send questions to The Exploratorium

The International Lyrics Server
http://www.lyrics.ch/

- lyrics from over 56,000 songs—rock, pop, oldies, folk, and more

Robot Information Central
http://www.robotics.com/robots.html

- links to everything you could ever imagine about robots from kids' toys to space probes

The Exploratorium's Ten Cool Sites!
http://www.exploratorium.edu/learning_studio/sciencesites.html

- 10 cool new sites each month (and an index of former ones) on arts, astronomy, chemistry, sciences, literature, drama, math, history, physics, psychology, weather, and more

Kids Connect
http://www.ala.org/ICONN/kidsconn.html

- Can't find a good site for your research project? Write a question online and a trained school librarian will respond within 48 hours giving you a good Internet address to look for information.

Heroes for Today
http://www.concord.k12.nh.us/schools/rundlett/heroes/

- a project by the students of a middle school in Concord, New Hampshire
- links to pages of information about many American heroes—Muhammad Ali, Arthur Ashe, Jimmy Carter, Amelia Earhart, Albert Einstein, Crazy Horse, Michael Jordan, Christopher Reeve, George Washington, and many more
- information about "Community Heroes"—how to get involved in local volunteer projects

Mawson Station, Antarctica
http://www.antdiv.gov.au/aad/exop/sfo/mawson/video.html

- pictures from the Australian research station at Mawson Station updated every hour during daylight hours
- map showing the location of the station
- current weather in Antarctica
- links to hourly pictures at other research stations

Link Sites

If the addresses listed above don't lead you to exactly the information you need for your research project, a good place to look is link sites. These sites are like the yellow pages of the phone book—they tell you where to go to get what you want. But they have a big advantage over the yellow pages. With a click of your mouse on the address that looks useful, you're there!

When you "shop" at link sites, be careful not to get lost. Some of them give you so many choices (and not always good choices) that you might feel overwhelmed. Look for addresses that seem like the best bets, and check out those sites.

Here are some of the best link sites that we found on the Web for middle school research projects.

Yahooligans: The Web Guide for Kids
http://www.yahooligans.com

Although this site was designed for kids 7 to 12 years old, many of the links lead you to quite sophisticated information. Information is very well organized, so it's easy to find what you're looking for. Even better, this site can be searched (not all sites can), which is a big time saver when you are doing research. A search for "wolf" came up with 18 recommended sites; a search for "Mars" came up with 52. Here are the categories:

- Around the world—countries, politics, history, holidays, travel, religions, cultures, geography, languages, U.S. states, and more
- Art soup—museums, drama, dance, crafts, photography, sculpture, architecture, art history, museums and galleries, and more
- Computers, games, and other online stuff
- Entertainment—TV, movies, music, magazines, theme parks, and more
- School bell—programs, homework helpers, careers, clubs and organizations
- Science and oddities—space, environment, dinosaurs, airplanes, chemistry, insects, physics, inventions, and animals
- Sports and recreation—scores, hobbies, trivia, horse races, volleyball, Frisbee, and karate
- The scoop—comics, newspapers, news magazines, and weather

Kids Web: A World Wide Digital Library for School Kids
http://www.npac.syr.edu/textbook/kidsweb

This site is excellent for research. It was designed for grades K-12 and has links to sites in these categories:

- art
- literature
- chemistry
- astronomy and science
- environmental science
- mathematics
- geography
- weather and meteorology
- history
- drama
- music
- computers
- biology and life sciences
- geology and earth sciences
- physics
- science and technology
- government
- sports

Berit's Best Sites for Children
http://db.cochran.com/db_HTML:theopage.db

This site, written primarily for younger middle schoolers, reviews hundreds of sites and gives each a rating (5/5 being the best). There are notes and descriptions of each site, helping you decide if it might be useful for your research. You can search within this site, so you could ask, for example, if there are good links to "aardvark," to "Alaska," or to whatever your topic might be. Included are these categories:

- astronomy
- health and safety
- art galleries
- science and math
- TV and movies
- fish and ships
- animals
- creepy crawlies (insects)

- environment
- government
- history
- world travel
- dinosaurs
- frogs
- sports and recreation

Just for Kids
http://www.eagle.ca/~matink/kids.html

There are no descriptions of the link sites, so it's a little hard to tell whether they will be useful for your research, but a search here might lead you to just what you need for your project. This site gives links in the following categories:

- animals
- space
- science and museums
- travel
- fun

- dinosaurs
- sports
- TV, radio, and music
- magazines and news

Rigby Kids' Places
http://www.reedbooks.com.au/rigby/kids/kidplace.html

This address includes good descriptions of the link sites. Included are the following:

- forces of nature and dinosaurs
- interesting places and maps
- arts, crafts, and music
- news, magazines, publishing
- fun, games, puzzles
- animals
- stories, TV, movies
- science and space
- the sea

AOL NetFind Kids Only
http://www.aol.com/search/kids/

Search the Internet for kid-friendly sites. Included are these categories:

- fun
- discover
- travel
- news
- interact
- sports

Route 6-16: The Safe Route on the Information Highway
http://www.microsys.com/616

This site leads you to a huge reference library with dictionaries, encyclopedias, and lots of information from the U.S. government. You can find links within these categories:

- math
- science
- world
- general
- space
- animals
- history
- art, poetry, music

INDEX